# Praise for *The Love Language of Flowers*

"A most elegant and timeless compendium for flower lovers. The gorgeous photography accompanied by heartfelt prose, the advice and wisdom, the recipes for arranging, and the meaning of flower varieties…this book is truly a genuine tribute to blooms and blossoms, and a guide I never knew I so desperately needed."

—**Angela Ferraro-Fanning**, founder of Axe & Root Homestead, author of *The Sustainable Homestead*

"The lost art of using flowers to express yourself is something Jess is bringing back to life. This book gives beautiful and practical information, inspiring us all to speak in a forgotten language. It's a welcome return to bringing magic back to not only special occasions, but also our everyday."

—**Bailey Van Tassel**, The Kitchen Garden Society

"*The Love Language of Flowers* is bursting with stunning photography and practical guides to elevate your own floral designs. It should be an essential addition to every flower lover's tool kit."

—**Graeme Corbett**, Bloom & Burn

"Jess has a magical way of capturing the fascinating world of botanicals, encouraging us into the garden and guiding us in creating beauty with gifts from nature. This book is enchanting to the eyes, inspiring for the mind, and refreshing for the soul."

—**Maggie Hyde**, Petal Back Farm

"A feast for the eyes, a spark to the mind, and a tug on the heart. Jess brings her wholly unique and stunning touch to the art of floral arrangements. A complete capture of simple beauty, and the power flowers evoke in us all."

—**Skye Hamilton**, Hamilton House Designs

"*The Love Language of Flowers* is sure to become a treasured resource of inspiration and technique for all those who find themselves called to create with nature's floral bounties. A book to enjoy alongside warm tea on cold winter days, as we wait for spring blossoms to allow us to put it to practical use."

—**Robyn Chubey**, Prairie Glow Acres

"Flowers are a language unto themselves, and they engage our senses on a different level. Whether we garden and work with them on a regular basis or we simply buy them to enjoy and create a mood or decorate a space, flowers are the perfect adornment and creative medium. *The Love Language of Flowers* is a visually captivating and soul-inspiring book that will put you in touch with the 'craft of making.' It will draw you into the timeless, creative space of using your hands to bring beauty to life. This book will inspire you in a multitude of ways as it provides you with the guidance, tools, and timeless wisdom to cultivate beautiful projects to love again and again."

—**Jan and Erin Johnson**, founders of Trailblazher Inc., publishers of *Trailblazher* magazine

"*The Love Language of Flowers* draws you in with stunning photography and keeps the reader engaged with an abundance of floral tips and tricks. Each page inspires gardeners and vintage lovers alike to create beautiful bouquets of their own. Cheers to Buttermore and McGuinness."

—**Penny Pennington Weeks**, gardener and blogger

# The Love Language of Flowers

# The Love Language of Flowers

Floriography and Elevated, Achievable,

Vintage-Style Arrangements

By Jess Buttermore and Lisa McGuinness

yellow pear 🍐 press

CORAL GABLES

Copyright © 2023 by Jess Buttermore and Lisa McGuinness.
Published by Yellow Pear Press, a division of Mango Publishing Group, Inc.

Cover Design: Elina Diaz
Cover & interior photos: Jess Buttermore
Layout & Design: Elina Diaz

For permission requests, please contact the publisher at:
Mango Publishing Group
2850 S Douglas Road, 2nd Floor
Coral Gables, FL 33134 USA
info@mango.bz

For special orders, quantity sales, course adoptions and corporate sales, please email the publisher at sales@mango.bz. For trade and wholesale sales, please contact Ingram Publisher Services at customer.service@ingramcontent.com or +1.800.509.4887.

The Love Language of Flowers: Floriography and Elevated, Achievable, Vintage-Style Arrangements

Library of Congress Cataloging-in-Publication number: 2023930429
ISBN: (print) 978-1-68481-191-5, (ebook) 978-1-68481-192-2
BISAC category code: GARDENING/Essays & Narratives

Printed in China

# Table of Contents

# Introduction

Flowers carry on dialogues through the graceful bending of their stems
and the harmoniously tinted nuances of their blossoms.

*—August Rodin*

In the Victorian era, flowers served as beautiful messengers that whispered what often could not be spoken aloud. They were the equivalent of clandestine text messages or notes of encouragement—a way to express friendship, pride, or feelings of love. They asked for reconciliation, requested secret meetings, offered compassion, and expressed desires. Flowers told the tale of hidden emotions during a time of extreme discretion. The key to decoding the meanings was found in oral tradition and flower dictionaries, which sometimes held varying definitions for specific flowers, which became known as *floriography* or the language of flowers.

Entwined in a bouquet, the meaning of flowers becomes even richer. One can express not just "love" with a single rose, but specific types of love, such as "passionate love" (page 161) or "maternal love" (page 147) as well as different sentiments like "grace" or "thankfulness." This book presents a multitude of arrangements imbued with a specific meaning and constructed with common flower varietals. You can easily build these arrangements at home using a few basic tools and tricks.

Also included are three floral glossaries to get you orientated. The first is arranged by common flower name so that as you select flowers or botanicals—whether in your garden or at a flower market—you can look up the meanings behind the blooms you admire. The second glossary is arranged by meaning, so you can easily access a list of flowers representing the sentiment you would like to express. And the third is arranged by season, so you can find the right flower when the time is right. The possible combinations are as abundant and diverse as the flowers in the fields. And who knows? These arrangements may even inspire what you grow in your garden.

The meanings in this book are as true as possible to the historical Victorian meanings. If a flower or botanical has conflicting or multiple meanings, we chose the meaning that was consistent through multiple sources. For the occasional flower or botanical associated with both a positive and negative meaning, we chose the positive meaning in the generous spirit of this book.

Because the blooming season of flowers is fleeting but important sentiments occur year-round, there will be occasions when the specific flower you desire to include in a bouquet is not available so each arrangement has a list of possible alternatives should you need them.

The arrangements in this book intentionally include flowers and botanicals that are easily available at flower markets, florists, and local shops. And don't forget to simply look outside your door. Your backyard garden may offer a bounty ready to become beautiful bouquet messengers. To add a contemporary twist, we have included elements such as succulents, herbs, and edibles in the bouquets. Feel free to "branch out" and include a variety of florals to create the bouquets of your dreams.

In addition to floriography, we have included floral-infused quotes, literary references, and lore to celebrate all things beautifully botanical.

# A Brief History of Floriography

There is no colour, no flower, no weed, no fruit, herb, pebble, or feather that has not a verse belonging to it: and you may quarrel, reproach, or send letters of passion, friendship, or civility, or even of news, without ever inking your fingers.

—*Lady Mary Wortley Montagu*

While the Victorians are credited with the term *floriography*, the practice of attributing meanings to blooms was first noted in the eighteenth century in the letters of Lady Mary Wortley Montagu (1682–1762). The wife of a British ambassador, Lady Montagu wrote about her life and travels throughout the Ottoman Empire. Noted in her letters was the practice she observed of flowers being used as a coded language to express a variety of sentiments including positive messages sharing love and devotion as well as the expression of negative thoughts such as distaste or dislike.

Later, during the Victorian era, the practice gained popularity as a way to communicate feelings in a time known for the requirement of extreme discretion. The first written compilation of the flower names and their meanings was published in 1819, in Charlotte de la Tour's *Le langage des fleurs*. The popularity spread, and this coded mode of communication became fashionable in Europe, England, and the United States through the nineteenth century.

Now, perhaps as a backlash to the onslaught of society's over-expression of every momentary thought through social media, the subtle language of flowers has come back into mode as messengers of sentiments not spoken or typed into texts but expressed through more refined and sensitive means.

Part One

# Toolbox

BUT FOR ONE'S
HEALTH AS YOU SAY,
IT IS VERY NECESSARY
TO WORK IN THE
GARDEN AND SEE THE
FLOWERS GROWING.

—Vincent Van Gogh

# Basic Materials

A host of tools are helpful to have on hand when creating a flower arrangement, but in a pinch, you can get by with three things: a vase, a pair of sharp scissors, and some tape (clear tape, masking tape, or even duct tape will work). That said, several other supplies come in handy and allow for more intricate flower arranging. To stock your floral "toolbox," pick up the following: several watertight vessels (of different sizes, shapes, and depths), a floral frog (preferably a few of varying shapes and sizes), garden snips, hand clippers for the garden to cut heavy stems, thorn stripping shears (to strip thorns off roses and other thorny stems), hammer, lighter, floral tape, floral wire (both a roll of lightweight wire for wrapping things like wreaths, and straight wire to help flowers stand tall and to create false stems), wooden skewers, paper to wrap bouquets (butcher or craft paper, newsprint, wrapping paper, or tissue paper), a roll of twine, a variety of ribbons to finish the presentation with a flourish, and tags and note cards to share the meaning and sentiment of your arrangement.

# Choosing Color

Many of the flowers used in the following arrangements come in an abundance of colors and sizes. When choosing colors within your arrangement, consider selecting flowers of similar shades and tones, as shown below. Limit yourself to two colors that complement each other. This means the two colors likely appear next to each other on the color wheel. If you want your blooms to stand out, choose a color different from the foliage. Let the foliage be your third color, acting as a neutral base for your arrangement. It is particularly lovely to gather blooms that are different shades of one color, as shown in the Enchantment arrangement on page 115. The shapes and textures offer visual interest to the arrangement without the distraction of competing colors.

# Conditioning

Conditioning flowers is the treatment of flowers and foliage after you've cut them from their root system or pulled them from the water bucket at your local farm stand or market. Because they are still living, they will continue to need food and water, so here are some tried and true techniques to prolong their beauty and vase life.

Bring a bucket half full of cold water with you when you gather your flowers. If you are harvesting from your garden, cut them early in the morning or late in the evening (just after sunrise or before sunset) to capture them at their strongest. Avoid cutting flowers in full sun or on hot days when flowers are most stressed. If choosing flowers from a market or farm stand, have a bucket of cold water ready to transport your beautiful stems home.

Choose blooms that are only partially opened without any browning or wilting petals. Blooms that are fully opened or starting their final fade, while beautiful, will begin to wilt and lose their petals quickly. Tulips should be closed when harvested or purchased, with only a hint of color showing. Daffodils, irises, peonies, and roses can also be harvested or purchased in bud form for the longest vase life. Flowers with long flowering stems, such as snapdragons and gladioli, should be purchased or harvested when the stem has a combination of buds and open flowers. For example, a gladiolus should have open flowers at the highest point of the stem and buds at the bottom. Snapdragons, on the other hand, will have open flowers on the bottom and buds at the top. Choosing a market bouquet that has a combination of buds and opened blooms will offer the most visual interest and range of sizes when creating your arrangement.

Open-faced flowers such as daisies, cosmos, and zinnias, should be purchased or harvested at their peak bloom, as they may not open if cut as buds.

Cut stems at a forty-five-degree angle to provide the largest surface space for your stems to drink. Immediately place them in the cold water. On hot days, add a few ice cubes, because even fifteen minutes without water can significantly impact blooms and botanicals. On the other hand, if you want your blooms to open more quickly, warm water will help.

Black-eyed Susans, chrysanthemums, oregano, stock, yarrow, and zinnia have a bad rap for turning their vase water a murky brown color in less than twenty-four hours. To remedy this, change the water daily and add a few drops of bleach to the water each time.

While most flowers need only the minimal conditioning described above, a few varieties of flowers and stems require additional attention:

- ✦ Lilacs should not be stored or arranged in a metal container. Doing so will cause them to wilt prematurely.

- ✦ Daffodils and hyacinths should not be arranged with other flowers, as they release harmful sap. Instead, let these beautiful spring blooms speak for themselves, creating interesting color combinations in their own bouquet.

- ✦ Marigolds are vibrant and plentiful during the summer months, but the scent can be a bit off-putting. To remedy this, mix a tablespoon of sugar into the water to neutralize the scent.

- ✦ Poppies, zinnias, sunflowers, and hollyhocks, among some other varieties of flowers, exude a milky substance from the bottom of their stems after being cut. Searing the ends of these types of flowers with a flame (match or lighter) will keep the plant's nutrients in while still allowing water to be absorbed through the rest of the sides of the stem.

- ✦ Always cut carnations just above one of the nodes (bumps on the stalk) to give them an easier opportunity to absorb water.

- ✦ The pollen on the stamens of lilies will stain. Before adding lilies to an arrangement, carefully clip off the stamens with your snips.

- ✦ All woody stems (flowers like lilac, camellias, and azaleas, or branches such as crab apple, cherry, or dogwood, for example) need to be frayed at the ends. To do this, cut the bottom of the stems about an inch vertically with a knife or clip with your snips. Then, if the branch is thick or tough, smash the bottom inch a couple of times with a hammer. This will loosen the fibers and allow the branch or stem to absorb water and nutrients easier.

# Support

There is more than one way to keep flowers from listing to the side of an arrangement. The most common method is the use of a floral frog. Frogs are usually heavy and flat on the underside and spikey or gridded on the top. When placed at the bottom of a bowl or vase, they can hold even the most unwieldy flowers firmly upright. To use, press the ends of the stems directly into the frog's spikes or slide them into the gridded holes to position them exactly where you want them. Use a bit of floral putty on the bottom of the flower frog if it moves around easily in your vessel. Secure the floral frog to the bottom before adding water. Putty will not adhere properly to a wet surface.

If you don't have a frog, a quick solution is to create a grid of tape across the top of the vessel in a crisscross pattern, leaving plenty of room between the lines of tape to hold stems in place. Again, do this before adding water so the tape properly adheres to the vase. When creating the arrangement, be sure to fill in some flowers or foliage around the edges to conceal the tape or carefully remove the tape after your arrangement is complete.

Wire mesh, often called chicken wire, is another simple way to secure stems in place. This is a low-cost, low-waste, recyclable option and is a great alternative to frogs for arrangements being gifted. While wearing gloves to protect your hands from the sharp edges of the wire ends, shape the wire into a ball and gently press it into your vessel so it is positioned just below the top lip of the vessel. Anchor the wire down with four pieces of tape in a crisscross formation secured to the rim of the vessel. Again, use flowers to conceal the mechanics.

If you appreciate the classic simplicity and accessibility of using various sizes of mason jars as vases, grid lid inserts are available as a low-cost, low-waste, and recyclable option to add stability. These metal grid lid inserts come in both regular and wide-mouth mason jar sizes and set on top of your mason jar before screwing on the metal ring. I've found that they fit even the most vintage mason jars.

One final tip for adding a quick support system to your vessel is to use the red mesh bags oranges often come in at the grocery store. This works best with mason jars because the metal ring can be used to secure it into place. If using a traditional glass vase or metal vessel, simply cut a piece large enough to cover a little beyond the opening and then secure it in place with a piece of tape that continues all the way around the vessel. Then, make sure to cover the mesh with foliage and low-situated blooms when building the arrangement to conceal the mesh.

# Stem Reinforcement

While none of the bouquets in this book have the stems reinforced—allowing their true floral nature to shine through—it's nice to know how to reinforce stems if you would like to. Getting thin, flimsy stems to stand straight can be a challenge. And, of course, top-heavy blooms can cause stems to bend under their weight. Fortunately, there is a simple solution to drooping stems, which is green floral tape. Even the most flexible stem can be made rigid with a solid wrapping of floral tape.

To apply the tape, grasp the stem directly under the blossom. Beginning at the top of the stem, wrap floral tape around it, gradually moving downward in a spiral pattern, being sure to slightly overlap the edge of the tape. Once you've reached the bottom of the stem, cut the tape and secure it onto itself. Another option is to place a length of floral wire alongside the stem and wrap the wire and stem together with floral tape. The two together will make even the floppiest flower stems stand soldierly.

# Mock Stems and Fruit Stems

Occasionally, an arrangement calls for a flower bloom that needs to be separated from its naturally occurring state. Gladiola blossoms are a perfect example—each stem produces many blossoms, but you may not want that many blooms so close together in an arrangement. If that's the case, you can create a "mock stem" for your bouquet using a length of floral wire and a strip of floral tape. Here's how: First, remove the blossom you'd like to include from its natural stem by either cutting or pinching it off at the base of the bloom. Next, push the floral wire through the bottom of the blossom horizontally (kind of like threading a needle). Push the wire through the flower until there's an equal amount of wire on each side of the bloom, then bend both sides of the wire down to form a "stem." Then, starting at the top, directly under the flower, begin to wrap the wire "stem" with floral tape, gradually moving downward in a spiral pattern, being sure to slightly overlap the edge of the tape. When you get to the end of the wire, cut the tape. Now you have a beautiful single bloom ready to join your bouquet. When using this technique, note that the life of the flower will be considerably shorter than one that can be kept in water.

Mock stems can also be added to fruit to give the arrangement a sense of abundance or extra color and texture. But not all fruit is handily created with a stem that will seamlessly fit into a floral arrangement. If you want to include something like figs, persimmons, pomegranates, plums, pears, or any other fruit that doesn't have a long stem, all you need are thin wooden skewers. When you are ready to tuck the fruit among the flowers, simply insert the skewer into the bottom or the top of the piece of fruit (depending on which side is more visually appealing) until it reaches the core. Then tuck the skewer "stem" into the arrangement and voilà! The fruit is now part of the arrangement. If the wooden skewer is visible, wrap it in green floral tape so it blends in with the stems of the other flowers in the bouquet.

The Love Language of Flowers

# Stripping Stems

Whether cutting flowers from a garden or purchasing them from a flower market, you will most likely need to tidy the stems so they will be easy to work with, look their most elegant and keep the water fresher. The key is to remove all foliage that would lie below the waterline. This will decrease bacteria growth in the water, helping to keep the water fresher for longer. If you aren't sure how much foliage to leave on, retain the leaves on the top third of the stems during the initial pruning. Begin by removing excessive leaves and torn, dried out, or otherwise unsightly leaves. You can remove leaves with scissors, clippers, thorn strippers, or by hand if they aren't too prickly. In addition, remove any thorns or prickles from the stems with either thorn strippers or hand clippers. Once the stems are cleaned up, they will be easier to work with. You can continue to remove additional foliage if needed as you place the stems in the bouquet.

## Reflexing Blooms

Reflexing is the simple technique of altering the shape and style of a single bloom to increase the size and impression of the bloom. This technique is most commonly and successfully used on roses but can be used on any blooms with multiple layers of petals that open outward from a single center. To begin, remove the guard petals, which are the outer and usually largest petals. They tend to be tougher, have damage, or are beginning to wilt. Next, take the outermost petals and gently fold them open using your thumb and index finger. Gingerly work around the rose, careful not to tear or crease the petals as you go. As you move into the third layer of petals, they will become stiffer and more difficult to reflex. Decide if the bloom looks full at this point. If you would like to keep reflexing, turn the stem upside down and roll the stem of the flower back and forth between your palms several times to gently loosen the tighter petals. You can also softly blow on the center-most part of the flower to help open it. Continue reflexing the flower until you are satisfied with the fullness of the bloom. Reflexing some but not all the blooms in your arrangement will also add visual interest and variations of size of one variety of flower.

## Vessel Varieties

Think outside the glass vase. Vases come in all shapes and sizes, and, with the addition of a frog, there are no limits to the watertight containers you can use for your arrangements. Antique or contemporary teapots, such as Japanese teapots, make beautiful vessels for flower arrangements, as do vintage bottles. Ribbon- or twine-wrapped tin cans, watering cans, garden pots, galvanized buckets, and wall vases can all be gorgeously filled with blooms. Glass, silver, stone, ceramic, and porcelain vessels work well for lovely floral bouquets, so keep arrangements in mind when browsing flea markets, boutique shops, and antique stores.

Your kitchen or the kitchenware section of your favorite home goods store is another place to find interesting vessels. Some examples include mason jars, water pitchers, mixing bowls, ceramic mugs, stoneware pestle and mortar sets, and flour and sugar kitchen canisters. Kitchenware as a vessel is an excellent way to give a gift that the recipient can use and appreciate after the flowers have faded.

When a vessel is not watertight, simply choose a watertight vessel that is slightly smaller in diameter and shorter in height, even if it is not the most attractive option. Examples of watertight vessels I've used for this situation include old glass vases, mason jars, and water glasses. I've also taken empty yogurt containers and pickle jars from my recycling bin, washed them and used them to hold the water and floral arrangement inside larger vessels such as baskets and leaky vintage pales. Place the smaller watertight vessel inside the larger vessel and add water before adding your support and building your arrangement. This system also works well for holding water inside hollowed-out pumpkins and gourds.

# Foliage as a Filler

When visualizing flower arrangements, remember that branches and leaves make striking additions to floral bouquets. To incorporate branches into your arrangement, clean up the stems as directed in the above Stripping Stems section and tuck the branches into the arrangement as desired. You can do this with twigs or branches of cedar, blue spruce, fir, dogwood, olive, cherry, cypris, pine (covered in pinecones), willow, cotton, tallow berry, bittersweet berry, and beauty berry. Simply gorgeous foliage such as ivy, ferns, lamb's ear, salal, salmonberry and raspberry foliage, wheat, eucalyptus, holly, and ornamental grasses also make beautiful additions to bouquets.

Herbs also make a gorgeous, fragrant, and useful filler. Basil, mint, lemon balm, calendula, rosemary, oregano, juniper, and sage are especially lovely additions to arrangements.

# Beyond Botanics

Take your arrangement to the next level by incorporating simple but elegant details of nontraditional elements. Edibles such as persimmons, apples, pears, grapes, figs, miniature pumpkins and gourds, snow peas or large unique-looking beans (i.e., lizard tongue) still on the vine, Chinese lanterns (a.k.a. ground cherries), vined grape tomatoes, lemons, and limes are all popular fruits for elements of interest and flair. Additionally, they are perfect for adorning the kitchen island or dinner table. Tips for creating stems for fruit can be found on page 28.

Substituting filler flowers and traditional foliage with leafy vegetables, such as rainbow Swiss chard, kale (traditional, ornamental, or flowering), and cabbage add texture and sophistication. Succulents, air plants, and moss are other unexpected foliage that will add a subtle but beautiful bohemian vibe to any arrangement.

Dried botanicals such as oats, wheat, lavender, hydrangea, strawflower, fox tail and bunny tail grasses, rose, daisies, yarrow, feverfew, and willow branches are other elements that can add a rustic or vintage accent to your arrangement in addition to texture and color during the months where fresh blooms are more difficult to source locally.

## Prolonging the Life of Your Arrangements

To prolong the vase life of your blooms and foliage, provide nourishment in the water. This can often be done using items you already have at home. I recommend adding a pinch of sugar, a splash of lemon-lime soda or a single aspirin (to add acid), or a drop of bleach (to prevent bacteria). The water temperature should be cold. On hot days, a few ice cubes can be added to the water to keep the blooms fresh. Lastly, flowers love fresh water daily. Cloudy water is a sign that bacteria is present in the water, which directly interferes with the stems' ability to draw in the nutrients and water it needs. When changing out the water, take a moment to retrim your stems by cutting a half inch or so from the bottom.

# Vase Life

The blooms and botanicals included in an arrangement will bring joy and meaning to your home or the home of someone you care about. But not all flowers remain fresh-looking for the same amount of time, which can be tricky when visualizing how long the bouquet or arrangement will stay beautiful. The good news is that as the blooms fade or the leaves begin to droop or discolor, those flowers can simply be plucked from the arrangement, while the still-fresh blooms can remain in the vase to let their beauty shine. With this in mind, here is a list of the average vase life ranges for many of the botanicals featured in this book.

- Air plants: over two months
- Alstroemeria: up to two weeks
- Anemone: seven to nine days
- Bachelor's Button: five to ten days
- Bee Balm: seven to ten days
- Bells of Ireland: seven to ten days
- Black-eyed Susan: seven to ten days
- Calendula: five to seven days
- Carnation: up to two weeks
- China Aster: seven to ten days
- Chrysanthemum: over two weeks
- Clematis: seven days in vase, at most
- Columbine: up to a week
- Cosmos: three to five days
- Dahlia: five days, at most
- Daisy, Gerbera: seven to ten days
- Delphinium: five days
- Dusty miller: seven to ten days
- Echinacea (coneflower): seven to ten days
- Eryngium (sea holly): one to two weeks
- Eucalyptus: over two weeks

- Fennel: five to seven days
- Fern: seven to ten days
- Feverfew: five to seven days
- Flowering branches: generally one week
- Freesia: up to one week, at most
- Fritillaria: five to seven days
- Gardenia: one to two days
- Geranium: over two weeks
- Geranium, scented: about a week
- Ginger: ten to fourteen days
- Gomphrena: over two weeks
- Grasses: about a week
- Heather: seven to ten days
- Heliotrope: over two weeks
- Hellebore: five days
- Hyacinth: three to seven days
- Hydrangea: five to nine days
- Ivy: up to two weeks
- Jasmine: five days
- Kale, ornamental: over two weeks
- Lamb's ear: four to five days

- Laurel: two to three weeks
- Lavender: five to seven days
- Leucojum: over two weeks
- Lemon balm: two or three days
- Lisianthus: up to two weeks
- Mint: seven to ten days
- Narcissus: five to seven days
- Nasturtium: a week
- Oregano: seven to ten days
- Pansy: five to seven days
- Peony: five to seven days
- Poppy: one to three days
- Protea: up to two weeks
- Queen Anne's Lace: five to seven days
- Ranunculus: seven to ten days
- Riceflower: ten to fourteen days
- Rose: five days

- Rosemary: over two weeks
- Sage: ten days or more
- Salix (French willow): over two weeks
- Scabiosa (pincushion): up to a week
- Snapdragon: seven to ten days
- St. John's wort buds: over two weeks
- Stock: five to seven days
- Strawflower: over a week
- Succulents: two or more months
- Sunflower: seven to ten days
- Sweet William: seven to ten days
- Sweetpea: four days
- Tulip: seven to ten days
- Veronica: five to seven days
- Willow branches: up to two weeks
- Yarrow: five days
- Zinnia: seven days

## Building Arrangements

When incorporating a single focal flower, it should be prominently displayed but needn't be perfectly centered. Often, positioning a single flower off to one side or lower than center is most appealing to the eye while adding subtle drama.

When building large arrangements, start with a base of foliage and a low-positioned focal flower, working your way up and out.

When choosing blooms at your market or in your garden, look for variations in size, hue, and open blooms versus buds within a single type of flower to entertain the eye. The more variation within one type of flower of the same color, the better.

# Hand-Tied Bouquets

The term "hand-tied" refers to the method by which a floral bouquet is constructed. It does not refer to the shape of the bouquet (such as posy, round, nosegay, or cascading); they can all be hand-tied. Spiraling the stems in handheld bouquets is not only beautiful but also adds space between the blooms, allowing them to "breathe," extending their beauty and life.

Before beginning, cut either a piece of twine or ribbon to secure the bouquet. Be sure it's long and then place the twine or ribbon over your shoulders so you know exactly where it is and can reach it when it's time to secure the arrangement.

To construct a hand-tied bouquet, begin by holding a single stem in one hand, and with the other hand, begin adding new stems on top at a slight angle, turning your bouquet 45 degrees (a quarter turn) as you add each new stem. Continue turning and adding stems to the bouquet until it is the size and shape you desire. After the bouquet is assembled, while still holding it in your hand, secure the bouquet's stems with twine or a rubber band.

If you would like your hand-tied bouquet to resemble those you see at flower markets, consider trying to incorporate what I call the "Five Fs." The first "F" is your focal flower. This is the bloom (or set of blooms) you want to showcase or that is the main ingredient in your meaningful ingredients list. Next, add a layer of filler (the second "F") and/or foliage (the third "F") around the focal flower. This can be a secondary flower (something that doesn't compete with the focal flower) and/or foliage to create breathing space between the blooms. Next, turn the bouquet 45 degrees as described previously and add a botanical that has flutter (the fourth "F"). When choosing a flutter stem, look for something soft and airy to add texture, vertical interest, and a level of whimsy. Examples are Queen Anne's lace, forget-me-nots, love-in-a-mist, bachelor buttons, columbine, flax, ornamental grasses, pincushions, wheat or oats, and lace flowers. Finally, turn the bouquet 45 degrees again and add the final "F" element: fragrance. Ensuring you have something aromatic in your bouquet will ignite all the senses for the most well-rounded arrangement. Continue turning and adding these five elements until your bouquet reaches the fullness desired.

# Ribbons and Wrappings

It's a nice touch to wrap arrangements in tissue, butcher paper, or kraft paper to give to neighbors, teachers, caregivers, and loved ones. The neutral paper color frames the bouquet so the recipient focuses on the botanical elements.

Here are three wrap options so you can find the one that best fits your occasion:

## Market Wrap

There are many ways to create the traditional market wrap fold; one of the easiest ways is to cut a piece of craft paper to eighteen inches square (approximately forty-five-cm square) for average-sized bouquets or eighteen inches by twenty-four inches (approximately forty-five cm by sixty cm) for larger bouquets. Cut a piece of twine or ribbon to approximately three to four feet (1.25 m) long.

Fold the paper once the long way (horizontally) to create your uneven "double mountain top" half-fold and then cut a two-inch (five-cm) slit in the middle of the folded edge. Next, fold the two pieces back to create a triangle shape cutout at the bottom as shown.

Place your hand-tied bouquet on top of the paper, center the stems down the arrow cutout, and then secure the bouquet with the twine or ribbon.

## Posy Wrap

This simple, beautiful wrap is perfect for gifting small flower arrangements. It is quick and easy and only uses tissue or kraft paper and twine.

Gather three pieces of tissue paper or one piece of craft paper, approximately fifteen by twenty inches (forty by fifty cm). Cut a piece of twine three feet (one m) long.

Fold to create two "mountains" (as shown below) with a flat horizontal bottom and then fold the right corner up vertically and press to create a crisp fold. Repeat for the left corner.

Next, lay your mini bouquet on top, pull the tissue paper around both sides of the bouquet, and secure it with twine at the "waist" where the bare stems begin or are secured together.

# Gift Wrap

This wrap is perfect for something a bit more elaborate. Begin by cutting three pieces of tissue paper three inches wider than the width of your bouquet. Also cut three pieces of twine between one and two feet (0.3 to 0.6 m) long.

Fold all three pieces of tissue paper in an uneven "double mountain top" half-fold. Wrap the first around the bouquet, giving slightly more backing to the left side. Then wrap the second around the bouquet, this time giving slightly more backing to the right side. Secure these two pieces of tissue with a piece of twine tied tightly into a bow.

Take the third piece of folded tissue paper and fold it again in the other direction and loosely fan it to create frill. Attach it to the front of the bouquet with twine, ensuring it does not obstruct the view of the flowers but frames them. Next, cut two pieces of kraft or wrapping paper to eighteen inches square (approximately forty-five cm square). Fold each piece into thirds vertically.

Position the first piece behind the bouquet, slanting it so that the point of the unfolded corner is upright and slightly to the left. Position the second piece behind the first, slanting it so that the point of the unfolded corner is upright and slightly to the right. Secure with twine and/or a ribbon bow.

If you can't find the type of ribbon you want at the craft store, you can make your own. DIY ribbon is simple and often free. If you have a favorite clothing item that is stained, your children have outgrown, or is no longer something you want to wear, it can be repurposed by cutting or tearing the fabric into long strips. If the fabric is difficult to tear, try cutting it the first inch to start and then see if it will tear from there. Two-inch wide (five cm) strips are a good size; however, thinner (one in/2.5 cm) strips will give a more subtle look and are best for smaller bouquets, while thicker fabric strips (three in/7.5 cm or wider) can be impactful for dramatic or large bouquets. If you don't have clothing items ready to be repurposed in this way, check your local thrift store for used table runners, table clothes, cotton sheets, or linen napkins.

# Share the Meaning

When giving a bouquet infused with a meaning you would like to share, be sure to include a note. The missive can be as simple and practical as a handwritten note on a kraft paper tag or as elaborate as a designed and printed card aesthetically integrated into the bouquet. The main point is to share the meaning of the botanicals you chose. If you included herbs or vegetables in your arrangement, you could include a simple culinary preparation tip or favorite family recipe. Or, including one of the literary quotes found in this book could be a perfect finishing touch. After all, you've carefully chosen blooms to convey a sentiment, so be sure the recipient will remember your message long after the flowers have faded. If you would like to print a sheet of these botanical message cards, go to:

## Developing Your Own Personal Style

One of the best parts of floral design is the endless ways one can mix
and match the various elements of color, texture, positioning, form,
and meaning of botanicals in an arrangement. This book provides
several tools and recipes to guide and inspire you on your floral
journey to elevate your love language with flowers. But do not hold
yourself too rigidly to rules and restrictions. Take risks. Be curious
about botanicals and techniques that are new to you. Through this
process, find what is most pleasing to your eye and what makes
your heart sing, allowing the process to develop your style.

Part Two

# The Glossaries

I MUST HAVE FLOWERS,
ALWAYS AND ALWAYS.

—*Claude Monet*

# Meanings and Emotions with Their Flower Name

## A

Abundance: grapevine, nasturtium

Admiration: amethyst, carnation, cuckoopint, daffodil, dianthus, lisianthus

Adoration: cuckoopint, dwarf sunflower, lisianthus

Affectation: cockscomb, juniper, pear blossom

Affection: dianthus, heliotrope (devoted affection), juniper, mossy saxifrage, pear, sorrel

Agreement: strawflower, phlox

Ambition: hollyhock

Amiability: white jasmine

Anticipation: forsythia, Japanese anemone

Appreciation: lisianthus

Argument: fig

Attachment: gorce, Indian jasmine

Attraction: eryngium/sea holly

Audacity: larch

## B

Bashfulness: peony

Bear together: snowberry/wax berry/white coral berry

Beauty: amaryllis (splendid beauty), charmelia (charming beauty), clematis (mental beauty), eryngium/sea holly (attraction), flower-of-an-hour/hibiscus trionum, French honeysuckle, glory flower, hibiscus (delicate beauty), orchid (refined beauty), ranunculus (rich in attractions), riceflower (everlasting beauty), rose of Sharon, stock/gillyflower (lasting beauty; always beautiful to me) variegated tulip (beautiful eyes), white hyacinth

Beware: rhododendron

Blessedness: bachelor button/cornflower

Blissful pleasure: sweet pea

Boldness: carnation

Bond (powerful): alstroemeria

Bravery: French willow, peony, oak, sweet William (gallantry), yarrow

Broken-hearted: red carnation

## C

Calmness: hydrangea

Charming: musk cluster rose, ranunculus/Persian buttercup (radiant with charm), white jasmine (amiability)

Cheerful: coreopsis, Gerber daisy, poinsettia (be of good cheer), yellow lily (gaiety)

Comfort: bee balm, scarlet geranium, pear, chamomile

Cleansing/cleanliness: hyssop

Compassion: elder, thrift

Confidence: liverwort, hepatica, polyanthus lilac

Connection: snowberry/wax berry/white coral berry

Constancy: bluebell, blue hyacinth, geranium

Courage: black poplar, borage, edelweiss, mullein (take courage), protea, red or burgundy astrantia, sweet William (gallantry)

Creativity: air plant

Cure of heartache: cranberry, yarrow

Curiosity: sycamore

## D

Declaration of love: pink, red, or white tulip

Delicate pleasure: sweet pea, cornflower/bachelor button (delicacy)

Desire: juniper
Destiny: camellia (my destiny is in your hands)
Devotion: alstroemeria, honeysuckle, lavender, Peruvian heliotrope
Dignity: clove, dahlia, elm, laurel-leaved magnolia, magnolia
Dispassion: hydrangea
Durability: dogwood

E

Elegance: acacia (pink or white), China aster, locust, pomegranate blossom, purple fritillaria, yellow jasmine
Enchantment: purple rose
Encouragement: golden rod, John Hopper rose, rudbeckia
Endurance: cedar
Energy in adversity: chamomile
Esteem: sage, spiderwort, alyssum
Everlasting: strawflower
Extravagance: poppy, blush poppy (fantastic extravagance)

F

Faithfulness: blue violet, passionflower, heliotrope, ornamental kale/crane
Fame: tulip
Fantasy: Queen Ann's lace
Fascination: orange rose, fern
Fate: flax, hemp
Felicity: sweet sultan
Fertility: calendula, geranium
Fidelity: sage, ivy, lemon blossom (fidelity in love), plum, spiderwort, strawberry tree, veronica
Folly: columbine
Foresight: holly, strawberry

Forgiveness: nemophelia/baby blue eyes, blue scilia, purple hyacinth
Freedom: air plant
Friendship: blue periwinkle, calendula, freesia (lasting friendship), ivy, oak leaf geranium, peppermint, zinnia (thoughts of an absent friend)

G

Gallantry: sweet William
Generosity: orange blossom
Gladness: myrrh, spring crocus (youthful gladness)
Glory: laurel
Good fortune: China aster
Good luck: belles of Ireland, sweet basil
Goodness: mercury
Grace: pink rose, pink astrantia, yellow jasmine
Gracefulness: yellow jasmine, white geranium, pink rose
Gratitude: bellflower/campanula, dianthus, lisianthus

H

Happiness: delphinium, dill (good spirits), mugwort, myrrh (gladness), spring crocus (youthful gladness), sweet sultan (felicity), yellow lily (gaiety)
Happiness (return of): lily of the valley
Happy love: bridal rose, white rose
Health/healing: calendula, feverfew, Iceland moss, lily of the valley (healing heartbreak), oat, purple echinacea/coneflower, yarrow
Heartbroken: red carnation
Hidden things found: witch hazel
Hidden love: motherwort
Hidden worth: coriander
Honesty: honesty/lunaria

Hope: almond blossom, bachelor button/
    cornflower (hope in love), China aster,
    cyclamen (hidden hope), hawthorn,
    spruce, snowdrop
Humility: bluebell, broom

## I

I cling to thee: wisteria
I live for thee: cedar leaf
I miss you: zinnia
I partake in your sentiments: China aster
I will still be waiting: astilbe
I will never forget you: forget-me-not
Imagination: lupine
Immortality: cedar, St. John's wort
Impermanence: cherry blossom
Independence: eryngium/sea holly
Infatuation: Niphetos rose
Innocence: Leucojum/summer snowflake,
    viola, white astrantia, white daisy, white lilac
    (youthful innocence)
Insincerity: foxglove
Inspiration: angelica

## J

Joy: tulip
Joy in love and life: calendula,
    cosmos, oregano
Joys to come: cape jasmine, wood
    sorrel, celandine
Justice: black-eyed Susan, chestnut, rudbeckia

## K

Kindness: flax, oat

## L

Let me go: pink striped carnation (I cannot
    be with you)
Lightheartedness: larkspur
Love: bachelor button/cornflower (hope in
    love), bridal rose (happy love), cabbage/
    cottage rose, China aster, honeysuckle,
    juniper (love me), lemon blossoms, Lily of
    the Nile (magical love), myrtle, pin cushion/
    scabiosa, pink dianthus, purple violet (filled
    with love), red chrysanthemum, red rose,
    rose, rose hip, salal (love of life), white rose
    (happy love), yellow tulip (hopeless love)
Love (ardent): gladiola (you pierce my heart)
Love (at first sight): coreopsis, purple lilac (first
    emotions of love), red chrysanthemum
Love (bonds of): honeysuckle
Love (capricious): lady's slipper
Love (declaration of): pink, red, or white tulip
Love (endless): baby's breath (love
    everlasting), gomphrena/globe amaranth
    (immortal love), heliotrope (eternal love)
Love (first emotions of): purple lilac
Love (hopeless) yellow tulip
Love (humble): fuchsia
Love (impetuous): nasturtium
Love (passionate): red rose
Love (perfect): tulip
Love (returned): lavender rose, ambrosia
Love (secret): motherwort, acacia, clove (I have
    loved you and you have not known it)
Love (wedded): ivy
Love of nature: magnolia
Loved life/loved one: salal
Loveliness: camellia (perfected loveliness),
    orange blossom (your purity equals your
    loveliness), white carnation, white hyacinth
    (unobtrusive loveliness)

Loyalty: lavender, nasturtium

## M

Majesty: fritillaria
Magnificent: bird-of-paradise
Maternal love: moss, wood sorrel
Message: iris
Mirth: saffron crocus
Modesty: calla lily, peach rose, viola, violet

## N

Never forget: blue periwinkle (tender recollection), calendula (remembrance), forget-me-not, pink carnation (I will always remember you), rosemary (remembrance), spearmint, strawflower (never-ceasing remembrance)
New beginning: butterfly bush, daffodil

## O

Overcome difficulties: hellebore, mistletoe

## P

Passion: azalea, bougainvillea, red metamorph marigold, red or burgundy astrantia, rose of Sharon, white dittany
Patience: China aster, dock, liatris, ox-eye daisy
Peace: chamomile, olive branch, pin cushion/scabiosa, poppy, sedum
Perfection: strawberry
Perplexity: love-in-a-mist
Persecution: checkered fritillaria
Perseverance: borage, canary grass, dogwood, euphorbia, liatris, ox-eye daisy, sedum, swamp/sweet magnolia
Persuasion: rose of Sharon, Syrian mallow/althaea frutex

Pleasure (dangerous): tuberose
Pleasure (blissful, delicate): sweet pea
Preference: apple, apple blossom, canary grass, pink geranium, rose
Prestige: salmonberry
Presumption: snapdragon, toadflax
Pride: amaryllis, fritillaria, gloxinia, hundred-leaved rose
Profit: cabbage
Prolific: fig
Promise (keep your): plum
Prosperity: allium, beech, laurel, wheat
Protection: eucalyptus, heather, hellebore, St. John's wort, white geranium, yarrow
Purity: Leucojum/summer snowflake, orange blossom (your purity equals your loveliness), pin cushion/scabiosa, star of Bethlehem, white astrantia, white lily, white sedum

## R

Rebirth: butterfly bush, St. John's wort
Reconciliation: hazel
Refinement: gardenia, orchid (refined beauty)
Refusal: striped carnation
Regard: daffodil
Relieve my anxiety: Christmas rose
Remembrance: blue periwinkle (tender recollection), calendula, pink carnation (I will always remember you), forget-me-not, rosemary, spearmint (never forget), strawflower (never-ceasing remembrance), white periwinkle (pleasures of your memory)
Remorse: raspberry
Renewal: lavender
Resilience: borage, chamomile (energy in adversity)
Respect: fritillaria

Return of happiness: lily of the valley
Riches: corn, wax flower
Royalty: basil, purple fritillaria

## S

Scandal: hellebore
Secrecy: peony, maidenhair fern
Secret love: honey flower, yellow acacia
Selflessness: succulent
Self-love: narcissus
Sensuality: Spanish jasmine
Separation: Carolina jasmine
Sincerity: fern, garden chervil, honesty
Strength: cedar, borage, gladiola (strength
    of character), fennel, ginger, purple
    echinacea/coneflower, red or burgundy
    astrantia, succulent
Success: laurel
Sweetness: white carnation, white lily,
    honeysuckle (sweetness of disposition)
Sympathy: balm, bee balm, calendula, lemon
    balm, thrift

## T

Temptation: apple blossom, quince
Tenacity: succulent
Thankfulness: bellflower/campanula, calendula
Think of me: pansy, white clover
Thinking of you: calendula, China aster
Tranquility: mugwort, sedum, stonecrop
Truth: anemone, chrysanthemum,
    white chrysanthemum

## U

Unchangeable: globe amaranth/gomphrena

## V

Victory: spirea, nasturtium (triumph,
    victory in war)
Virtue: African violet, honeymelon sage (sweet
    virtue), mint, sage

## W

Waiting: astilbe
Warmth: feverfew, peppermint, spearmint
    (warmth of sentiment)
Wealth: purple fritillaria, wax flower
Welcome: wisteria
Wisdom: China aster (gained
    wisdom), columbine
Womanhood: pink astrantia
Worthy beyond beauty: alyssum
Worthy of praise: fennel

## Y

Youthful gladness: crocus
Youthful innocence: white lilac
Youthfulness: pink astrantia, Leucojum/
    summer snowflake (memory of youth)

## Z

Zest: lemon, lemon blossom
Zest for love: salal

## FORGET-ME-NOT

*True Love*

From off her glowing cheek, she sate and stretched
The silk upon the frame, and worked her name
Between the leaves, and Forget-me-not—
Her own doth her own auburn hair!
That Eve... sweet spring return,
...ile, her look,
...hful moo...

# Flower Names with Their Meanings and Emotions

## A

Acacia: chaste love, secret love

Acacia (pink or white): elegance

Acacia (yellow): secret love

Air plant: freedom, creativity

Allium: prosperity

Almond blossom: hope

Alstroemeria: devotion, powerful bond

Alyssum: esteem, worthy beyond beauty

Amaryllis: pride, splendid beauty

Amaranth (globe)/gomphrena: unchangeable, immortal love, endless love

Ambrosia: love returned

Amethyst: admiration

Anemone: forsaken, truth

Anemone (Japanese): anticipation

Angelica: inspiration

Apple: temptation, preference

Apple blossom: preference

Aster (China): patience, elegance, hope, love, valor, gained wisdom, good fortune, think of you

Astilbe: I will still be waiting

Astrantia (pink): womanhood, youth, grace

Astrantia (red, burgundy): strength, passion, courage

Astrantia (white): innocence, purity

Azalea: fragility, fragile passion, romance, temperance, ephemeral passion

## B

Baby's breath: love everlasting

Bachelor button/cornflower: blessedness

Basil: royalty, kingly

Basil, sweet: good wishes

Bee balm: comfort, sympathy

Beech tree: prosperity

Bells of Ireland: good luck

Bird-of-paradise: magnificence

Black poplar: courage

Black-eyed Susan: justice

Bluebell: constancy, humility

Borage: courage, bluntness, strength, perseverance, resilience

Bougainvillea: passion

Bridal rose: happy love

Broom: humility

Butterfly bush: rebirth, resurrection, new beginning

## C

Cabbage: profit

Calendula: healing, health, sympathy, thinking of you, thankfulness, joy, friendship

Calla lily: modesty

Camellia: my destiny is in your hands, perfected loveliness

Campanula/bellflower: gratitude

Canary grass: perseverance

Carnation: admiration, boldness, alas for my poor heart

Carnation (pink): I will always remember you

Carnation (pink striped): refusal

Carnation (red): my heart breaks

Carnation (striped): refusal

Carnation (white): sweet and lovely

Carnation (yellow): disdain

Cedar: strength, endurance, eternal life and immortality

Celandine: joys to come

Chamomile: resilience, energy in adversity, comfort, rest, peace

Charmelia: charming beauty

Cherry blossom: impermanence, beauty, female power

Chervil (garden): sincerity

Chestnut: justice

China aster: patience, elegance, hope, love, valor, gained wisdom, good fortune, think of you

Chrysanthemum: truth, love, "you can trust my love," perfection

Chrysanthemum (red): Love

Chrysanthemum (yellow): slighted love

Chrysanthemum (white): truth

Clematis: mental beauty

Clove: secret love (I have loved you and you have not known it), dignity

Clover (red): industry

Clover (white): think of me

Cockscomb: affectation

Columbine: folly, dreams, visions, wisdom

Columbine (purple): resolution, resolve to win

Coneflower/purple echinacea: strength, health

Coreopsis: cheerful, love at first sight

Coriander/flowering cilantro: hidden worth

Corn: riches

Cornflower/bachelor button: blessedness, delicacy, hope in love

Cosmos: joy in love and life

Cranberry: cure for heartache

Crocus (saffron): beware of success, mirth

Crocus (spring): youthful gladness, lasting devotion, cheerfulness

Cuckoopint: admiration

Cyclamen: hidden hope, diffidence

## D

Daffodil: admiration, new beginning, regard

Dahlia: dignity, everlasting commitment

Daisy (Gerbera): cheerful

Daisy (ox-eye): patience, perseverance

Daisy (white): innocence

Delphinium: happiness, levity

Dianthus: love, affection, gratitude, admiration (see also: carnation, sweet William)

Dill: good spirits

Dittany (white): passion

Dock: patience

Dogwood: perseverance, undiminished love, durability

## E

Echinacea/coneflower (purple): strength, health

Edelweiss: courage

Elder: compassion

Elm: dignity, patriotism

Eryngium/sea holly: independence, attraction

Eucalyptus: protection

Euphorbia: perseverance

## F

Fennel: worth of praise, strength

Fern: sincerity

Fern (maidenhair): secrecy

Feverfew: warmth, good health, you light up my life

Fig: prolific, argument

Flax: kindness, fate

Flower-of-an-hour (hibiscus trionum): beauty

Forget-me-not: forget me not

Forsythia: anticipation

Foxglove: insincerity, ambitious for you rather than for myself, "death bells"

Freesia: lasting friendship

French willow/salix: bravery

Fritillaria: respect, majesty, pride and power, persecution

Fritillaria (purple): wealth, royalty, elegance

Fuchsia: humble love

## G

Gardenia: refinement, purity and sweetness

Geranium: constancy, fertility, friendship, returning joy, protection, gentility, peace of mind

Geranium (oak leaf): friendship

Geranium (pink): preference

Geranium (scarlet): comfort

Geranium (white): gracefulness, protection

Gillyflower/stock: lasting beauty, you will always be beautiful to me

Gladiolus: strength (of character), ardent love (you pierce my heart), strength of character

Globe amaranth/gomphrena: unchangeable

Glory flower: gorgeous beauty

Gloxinia: pride

Goldenrod: encouragement

Gomphrena/globe amaranth: unchangeable, immortal love, endless love

Gorse: attachment

Grapevine: abundance

## H

Hawthorn: hope

Hazel: reconciliation

Heather: protection

Heliotrope: devoted affection, faithfulness, eternal love

Hellebore: protection, overcome scandal and slander

Hemp: fate

Hepatica: confidence

Hibiscus: delicate beauty

Holly: foresight

Hollyhock: ambition

Honesty/lunaria: honesty

Honey flower: secret love

Honeysuckle: bonds of love, devotion, sweetness of disposition

Honeysuckle (French): beauty

Hyacinth: sorrow

Hyacinth (blue): constancy, sincerity

Hyacinth (purple): forgiveness, sorrow

Hyacinth (red or pink): playfulness, sportiness

Hyacinth (white): beauty, unobtrusive loveliness

Hydrangea: calm, dispassion

Hyssop: cleansing, cleanliness

## I

Iris: message

Ivy: fidelity, friendship, wedded love

## J

Jasmine: grace, elegance

Jasmine (Cape): joys to come

Jasmine (Carolina): separation

Jasmine (Indian): attachment

Jasmine (Spanish): sensuality

Jasmine (white): amiability

Jasmine (yellow): elegance, grace

Juniper: affection, desire, love me

## K

Kale, ornamental: faithfulness

## L

Lady's slipper: capricious love

Larch: audacity

Larkspur: lightheartedness

Laurel: success, glory, prosperity

Lavender: renewal, devotion, loyalty

Lemon balm: sympathy

Lemon blossom: zest, fidelity in love

Leucojum/summer snowflake: memory of youth, purity, innocence

Liatris: patience, perseverance (I will try again)

Lilac (purple): first emotions of love

Lilac (white): youthful innocence

Lily (white): purity, sweetness

Lily (yellow) falsehood, gaiety

Lily of the Nile: magical love

Lily of the Valley: return of happiness, healing heartbreak

Lisianthus: appreciation, admiration, adoration, grateful for you

Liverwort: confidence

Locust: elegance

Love-in-a-mist: perplexity

Lupine: imagination

## M

Magnolia: dignity

Magnolia (laurel-leaved): dignity

Magnolia (swamp, sweet): perseverance

Marigold: uneasiness, grief, resurrection

Marigold (French): jealousy

Marigold (red metamorph): passion

Mercury: goodness

Mint: virtue

Mistletoe: I surmount difficulties

Moss: maternal love

Moss (Iceland): health

Mossy saxifrage: affection

Motherwort: concealed love

Mugwort: tranquility, happiness

Myrrh: gladness

Myrtle: love

## N

Narcissus: self-love, egotism

Nasturtium: abundance, impetuous love, loyalty, patriotism, triumph, victory in war

Nemophelia/baby blue eyes: forgiveness

## O

Oak: bravery

Oat: kindness, health, improvement, the witching soul of music

Olive: peace

Orange blossom: generosity, your purity equals your loveliness

Orchid: refined beauty

Oregano: joy in love and life; soothing, banish sadness

## P

Pansy: think of me, thoughts

Passionflower: faithfulness

Pear blossom: affection

Pear: comfort

Peony: bravery, bashfulness, secrecy

Periwinkle (blue): friendship, tender recollection

Periwinkle (white): pleasures of your memory

Phlox: agreement

Pincushion/scabiosa: purity, love, peace

Plum: fidelity, keep your promises

Poinsettia: be of good cheer

Poppy: extravagance, peace

Poppy (blush): fantastic extravagance

Primrose: early youth, first love, silent love

Protea: courage

## Q

Queen Anne's lace: fantasy

Quince: temptation

## R

Ranunculus/Persian buttercup: radiant with
    charm, rich in attractions
Raspberry: remorse
Rhododendron: danger, beware
Riceflower: everlasting beauty
Rose, rosehip: love
Rose (cabbage, cottage): ambassador of
    love, love
Rose (Christmas): relieve my anxiety
Rose (hundred-leaved): pride
Rose (John Hopper): encouragement
Rose (lavender): love returned
Rose (musk cluster): charming
Rose (Niphetos): infatuation
Rose (orange): fascination, desire, enthusiasm
Rose (peach): modesty
Rose (pink): grace, perfect happiness
Rose (pink, deep): gratitude
Rose (purple): enchantment, love returned
Rose (red): passionate love
Rose (white): happy love, worthiness,
    "you're heavenly," wisdom, charm,
    sympathy, secrecy
Rose (yellow): decrease of love, jealousy,
    friendship and joy
Rose of Sharon: beauty, mildness, passion,
    persuasion
Rosemary: remembrance
Rudbeckia/gloriosa daisy: justice,
    encouragement

## S

Saffron crocus: mirth, beware of success
Sage: virtue
Sage (honeymelon): sweet virtue
Salal: zest for love, loved life
Salix/French willow: bravery

Salmonberry: prestige
Scabiosa/pincushion: purity, love, peace
Sea holly/eryngium: independence, attraction
Sedum: peace, tranquility,
    perseverance, calmness
Sedum (white): purity
Snapdragon: presumption, graciousness,
    courteousness, luck in marriage
Snowberry/wax berry/white coral berry: bear
    together, connection, interweaving
Snowdrop/Galanthus: hope
Sorrel: affection
Sorrel (wood): joys to come, maternal love
Spearmint: warmth of sentiment, never forget
Spiderwort: esteem, fidelity
Spirea: victory
Spruce: hope
St. John's wort: protection, rebirth, immortality
Stock/gillyflower: lasting beauty, you will
    always be beautiful to me
Strawberry: foresight, perfection
Strawflower: agreement, everlasting
Succulent: tenacity, strength, selflessness
Sunflower (tall): haughtiness
Sunflower (dwarf): adoration
Sweet pea: blissful pleasure, delicate pleasure,
    thank you for a lovely time
Sweet sultan: felicity
Sweet William (dianthus): gallantry
Syrian mallow/althaea frutex: persuasion

## T

Thrift: compassion, sympathy
Tuberose: dangerous pleasure
Tulip: joy, perfect love
Tulip (pink, red, white): declaration of love
Tulip (variegated): beautiful eyes
Tulip (yellow): hopeless love

## V

Veronica: fidelity
Viola: innocence, modesty, decency
Violet (African): virtue
Violet (purple): filled with love, modesty

## W

Wax flower: enduring wealth, riches
Wheat: prosperity
Willow (French)/salix: bravery
Wisteria: welcome, I cling to thee
Witch hazel: hidden things found

## Y

Yarrow: cure for a broken heart, sacred,
    protection, healing, power, bravery

## Z

Zinnia: I miss you, thoughts of an absent friend

# Flower Names by Season

Bloom times can vary based on varieties, climate, and geographical location. Even within certain flowers, you may find a variation of when they bloom. Your local garden centers are an excellent resource for the bloom times in your region. Also, you may find flowers available to purchase that are sourced from other regions or even other countries when it may not be the bloom time in your area. Branches, grasses, and some flowers can be dried and used year-round. Those are noted in both seasons.

## Spring-Summer

### A

Acacia: chaste love, secret love

Acacia (pink or white): elegance

Acacia (yellow): secret love

Air plant: freedom, creativity

Allium: prosperity

Alstroemeria: devotion

Alyssum: esteem, worth beyond beauty

Ambrosia: love returned

Amethyst: admiration

Anemone: forsaken

Angelica: inspiration

Apple: temptation, preference

Apple blossom: preference

Aster (China): patience, elegance, hope, love, valor, gained wisdom

Astilbe: I will still be waiting

Astrantia (pink): womanhood, youth, grace

Astrantia (red, burgundy): strength, passion, courage

Astrantia (white): innocence, purity

Azalea: fragile, temperance, ephemeral passion

### B

Baby's breath: love everlasting

Bachelor button (cornflower): single blessedness

Balloon flower: endless love, honesty, obedience, desire for friend to return

Basil: royalty, kingly

Basil, sweet: good wishes

Bee balm: sympathy

Beech tree: prosperity

Bellflower (campanula): gratitude

Belles of Ireland: good luck

Bird-of-paradise: magnificence

Black-eyed Susan: justice

Black poplar: courage

Bluebell: constancy, humility

Borage: courage, strength, perseverance, resilience

Bridal rose: happy love

Broom: humility

Bougainvillea: passion

Butterfly bush: rebirth, resurrection, new beginning

### C

Calendula: healing, health, sympathy, thinking of you, thankfulness, joy, friendship

Calla lily: modesty

Camellia: my destiny is in your hands

Campanula (bellflower): gratitude

Canary grass: perseverance

Carnation: admiration, boldness

Carnation (pink): I will always remember you

Carnation (pink striped): refusal

Carnation (red): my heart breaks

Carnation (white): sweet and lovely

Cedar: strength, endurance, eternal life, immortality

Celandine: joys to come

Chamomile: resilience, energy in adversity

Charmelia: charming beauty

Cherry blossom: impermanence

Chervil (garden): sincerity

Clematis: mental beauty

Clove: I have loved you and you have not known it

Clover (red): industry

Clover (white): think of me

Cockscomb: affection

Columbine: folly

Columbine (purple): resolution

Campanula (bellflower): gratitude

Cedar: strength, endurance, eternal life, immortality

Cockscomb: affection

Coneflower (echinacea) (purple): strength, health

Coreopsis: cheerful

Coriander (flowering cilantro): hidden worth

Corn: riches

Cornflower (bachelor button): blessedness

Cosmos: joy in love and life

Crocus (spring): youthful gladness

Cuckoopint: admiration

Cyclamen: hidden hope, diffidence

Cynoglossum (hound's tongue): hope

## D

Daffodil: admiration, new beginning, regard

Dahlia: dignity

Daisy (white): innocence

Delphinium: happiness, levity

Dianthus: love, affection, gratitude, admiration (see also Carnation and Sweet William)

Dill: good spirits

Dittany (white): passion

Dock: patience

Dogwood: perseverance, undiminished love, durability

## E

Echinacea (purple) (coneflower): strength, health

Edelweiss: courage

Elder: compassion

Elm: dignity

Eryngium (sea holly): independence, attraction

Eucalyptus: protection

## F

Fennel: strength, worthy of all praise

Fern: sincerity

Fern (maidenhair): secrecy

Feverfew: warmth, good health, you light up my life

Fig: prolific, argument

Flax: I feel your kindness

Flower-of-an-hour (hibiscus trionum): beauty

Forget-me-not: forget me not

Forsythia: anticipation

Foxglove: insincerity, ambitious for you rather than for myself, "death bells"

Freesia: lasting friendship

Fritillaria: respect, majesty, pride and power, persecution

Fritillaria (purple): wealth, royalty, elegance

Fuchsia: humble love

## G

Gardenia: refinement
Geranium: constancy, fertility, friendship,
    returning joy, protection
Geranium (oak leaf): friendship
Geranium (scarlet): comfort
Geranium (white): gracefulness
Gardenia: refinement
Gerbera daisy: cheerful
Ginger: strength
Gladiolus: strength (of character), ardent love
    (you pierce my heart)
Globe amaranth (gomphrena): unchangeable,
    immortal love, endless love
Glory flower: glorious beauty
Gloxinia: pride
Gomphrena (globe amaranth): unchangeable,
    immortal love, endless love
Gorse: attachment
Grapevine: abundance

## H

Hawthorn: hope
Heather: protection
Heliotrope: devoted affection, devotion
Hepatica: confidence
Hibiscus: delicate beauty
Hollyhock: ambition
Honesty (lunaria): honesty, sincerity
Honeysuckle: bonds of love, devotion
Honeysuckle (French): beauty
Hyacinth (blue): constancy
Hyacinth (purple): forgiveness
Hyacinth (white): beauty,
    unobtrusive loveliness
Hydrangea: calm, dispassionate
Hyssop: cleansing, cleanliness

## I

Iris: message
Ivy: fidelity, friendship, wedded love

## J

Jasmine (Cape): joys to come
Jasmine (Carolina): separation
Jasmine (Indian): attachment
Jasmine (Spanish): sensuality
Jasmine (white): amiability
Jasmine (yellow): elegance, grace
Juniper: affection, desire, love me

## K

Kale, ornamental: faithfulness

## L

Lady's slipper: capricious love
Larch: audacity
Laurel: success, glory, prosperity
Lavender: renewal, devotion, loyalty
Lemon balm: sympathy
Lemon blossom: fidelity in love, love, zest
Leucojum/summer snowflake: memory of
    youth, purity, innocence
Lilac: first emotions of love
Liatris: patience, perseverance (I will try again)
Lily of the Nile: magical love
Lily of the valley: return of happiness,
    healing heartbreak
Linaria: presumption
Lisianthus: appreciation, admiration,
    adoration, grateful for you
Love-in-a-mist: perplexity
Lupine: imagination

## M

Magnolia: dignity
Magnolia (swamp, sweet): perseverance
Marigold: resurrection
Marigold (red metamorph): passion
Mercury: goodness
Mint: virtue
Mock orange: deceit
Moss: maternal love
Moss (Iceland): health
Mossy saxifrage: affection
Motherwort: concealed love
Mugwort: tranquility, happiness
Mullein: take courage
Myrrh: gladness
Myrtle: love

## N

Narcissus: self-love
Nasturtium: abundance, impetuous love, loyalty, patriotism, triumph, victory in war, conquest
Nemophila (baby blue eyes): forgiveness

## O

Oak: bravery
Oat: health
Olive: peace
Orange blossom: generosity, your purity equals your loveliness
Orchid: refined beauty
Oregano: joy in love and life, soothing, banish sadness
Ox-eye daisy: patience, perseverance

## P

Pansy: think of me
Passionflower: faithfulness

Pear blossom: affection
Pear: comfort
Peony: bravery, bashfulness, secrecy
Peppermint: friendship, warmth
Periwinkle (blue): friendship, tender recollection
Periwinkle (white): pleasures of your money
Pincushion (scabiosa): purity, love, peace
Plum: fidelity, keep your promise
Pomegranate blossom: elegance
Poplar (black): courage
Poppy: extravagance, peace
Poppy: fantastic extravagance
Protea: courage

## Q

Queen Anne's lace: fantasy
Quince: temptation

## R

Ranunculus/Persian buttercup: radiant with charm, rich in attractions
Raspberry: remorse
Rhododendron: danger, beware
Rice flower: everlasting beauty
Rose, rosehips: love, preference
Rose (cabbage, cottage): ambassador of love, love
Rose (hundred-leaved): pride
Rose (John Hopper): encouragement
Rose (lavender): love returned
Rose (musk cluster): charming
Rose (Niphetos): infatuation
Rose (orange): fascination
Rose (peach): modesty
Rose (pink): grace
Rose (purple): enchantment, love returned
Rose (red): passionate love

Rose (white): happy love, worthiness

Rosemary: remembrance

Rose of Sharon: beauty, mildness, passion, persuasion

Rudbeckia (gloriosa daisy): justice, encouragement

## S

Sage: virtue

Sage (honeymelon): sweet virtue

Sage: esteem, fidelity

Salal: zest for love, loved life, loved one

Salix (French willow): bravery

Salmonberry: prestige

Scabiosa (pincushion): purity, love, peace

Sea holly (eryngium): independence, attraction

Sedum: peace, tranquility, perseverance, calmness

Sedum (white): purity

Sorrel: affection

Sorrel (wood): joys to come, maternal love

Spearmint: warmth of sentiment, never forget

Spiderwort: esteem, fidelity

Spirea: victory

Spruce: hope

St. John's wort: protection, rebirth, immortality

Star of Bethlehem: purity, innocence

Stock (gillyflower): lasting beauty, you will always be beautiful to me

Stonecrop: tranquility

Strawberry: foresight, perfection, fidelity

Strawflower: agreement, everlasting

Succulent: tenacity, strength, selflessness

Sunflower (tall): haughtiness

Sunflower (dwarf): adoration

Sweet pea: delicate pleasure, blissful pleasure

Sweet William: gallantry

## T

Thrift: sympathy, compassion

Tuberose: dangerous pleasure

Tulip: joy, perfect love

Tulip (white, pink): declaration of love

## V

Veronica: fidelity

Viola: innocence, modesty, decency

Violet: faithfulness, worth, filled with love

## W

Wax flower: enduring wealth, riches

Wisteria: I cling to thee, welcome

Willow (French) (salix): bravery

Wisteria: welcome, I cling to thee

## Y

Yarrow: cure for a broken heart, sacred, war, protection, healing, power, bravery

## Z

Zinnia: I mourn your absence, thoughts of you

## Fall-Winter

## A

Acacia: chaste love, secret love

Acacia (pink or white): elegance

Acacia (yellow): secret love

Air plant: freedom, creativity

Almond blossom: hope

Alyssum: esteem, worth beyond beauty

Amaranth (globe): unchangeable

Amaryllis: pride

Ambrosia: love returned

Amethyst: admiration

Anemone (Japanese): anticipation

## B

Bellflower (campanula): gratitude
Bird-of-paradise: magnificence
Black poplar: courage
Bougainvillea: passion

## C

Campanula (bellflower): gratitude
Canary grass: perseverance
Cedar: strength, endurance, eternal life, immortality
Chestnut: justice
Chrysanthemum: truth
Chrysanthemum (red): love at first sight
Chrysanthemum (yellow): slighted love
Cockscomb: affectation
Cranberry: cure for heartache
Crocus (saffron): beware of success, mirth
Cyclamen: hidden hope, diffidence

## D

Dahlia: dignity
Dittany (white): passion
Dock: patience

## E

Eryngium (sea holly): independence, attraction

## F

Fern: sincerity
Fern (maidenhair): secrecy

## G

Globe amaranth (gomphrena): unchangeable, immortal love, endless love
Goldenrod: encouragement

Gomphrena (globe amaranth): unchangeable, immortal love, endless love
Gorse: attachment
Grapevine: abundance

## H

Hazel: reconciliation
Hellebore: protection, overcome scandal and slander
Holly: foresight
Honey flower: secret love
Hyssop: cleansing, cleanliness

## I

Ivy: fidelity, friendship, wedded love

## J

Juniper: affection, desire, love me

## K

Kale, ornamental: faithfulness

## L

Larkspur: lightheartedness
Laurel: success, glory, prosperity
Liatris: patience, perseverance (I will try again)
Lisianthus: appreciation, admiration, adoration, grateful for you
Liverwort: confidence

## M

Marigold: resurrection
Marigold (red metamorph): passion
Mercury: goodness
Mint: virtue
Mistletoe: I surmount difficulties
Moss: maternal love
Moss (Iceland): health

Mossy saxifrage: affection
Mugwort: tranquility, happiness
Mullein: take courage

## O

Oak: bravery
Oat: health
Olive: peace

## P

Poinsettia: be of good cheer
Protea: courage

## R

Rosehip: love, preference
Rosemary: remembrance

## S

Salal: zest for love, loved life, loved one
Sea holly (eryngium): independence, attraction
Snowberry (wax berry): bear together,
    connection, interweaving
Snowdrop: hope
Sorrel (wood): joys to come, maternal love
Spruce: hope
Stonecrop: tranquility
Succulent: tenacity, strength, selflessness
Sunflower (tall): haughtiness
Sunflower (dwarf): adoration

## V

Veronica: fidelity

## W

Wax flower: enduring wealth, riches
Wheat: prosperity
Willow (French): bravery
Witch hazel: hidden things revealed

Part Three

# The Arrangements

There are always flowers
for those who want
to see them.

—Henri Matisse

The sunflower turned
from the south to a fierce
light, not solar—
a rushing, red, cometary-
light—hot on vision and
to sensation.

—*Charlotte Bronte*

# ADORATION

"A splendid blossom of art and industry," said one, "has unfolded itself in the Champ de Mars, a gigantic sunflower, from whose petals one can learn geography and statistics, and can become as wise as a lord mayor, and raise one's self to the level of art and poetry, and study the greatness and power of the various lands."

—Hans Christian Anderson

The bright, lively sunflowers in this arrangement mirror the vibrant emotion of adoration and their branching, dainty blooms make them ideal for containers and gift-giving. Sunflower blooms follow the sun throughout the day in the same way we tend to focus on the people we adore, no matter where they are in the room. Combine dwarf sunflowers of different hues to symbolize that those we adore are admired not for one quality but a unique combination of characteristics. (Be sure to only use dwarf varieties, as tall sunflowers mean "haughtiness"!) "Abundance" is introduced with nasturtium because when we adore someone, it's effusive and the two botanicals not only bloom at the same time but truly complement each other in the floral world. Give this bouquet to someone you adore.

## Ingredients

**Adoration:** seven stems Topolino
dwarf sunflower
**Abundance:** five trailing stems nasturtium,
mixed colors

*Alternative botanicals:* amethyst, carnation,
cuckoopint, dianthus, feverfew, heliotrope,
juniper, lisianthus, pear, sage, sorrel

## To Create the Arrangement

1.  Choose a medium-sized vessel and fill it three-quarters full of water.

2.  Add a sphere of chicken wire to support the stems. (If you don't have chicken wire, see other plant support options on pages 25-26.)

3.  Next add the nasturtium, allowing it to cascade down the side. Include some stems that are stronger and straight to mingle with the sunflowers.

4.  Add the sunflowers, stem by stem, and allow them to rest where they want to so the arrangement has an organic, natural feel.

> *Tip: Choose blossoms that are in season in your region. They will be easier to find, more cost-efficient, and keep your arrangement from feeling outdated.*

The dry
eucalyptus
seeks god in the
rainy clouds.

—Wallace Stevens

# APPRECIATION

Roses and gladiolas make up bright mounds

Of flowers, with juniper and aniseed;

While sage, all newly cut for this great need,

Covers the Persian carpet that is spread

Beneath the table, and so helps to shed

Around a perfume of the balmy spring.

—*Victor Hugo*

Recognizing enjoyment and the feeling of being grateful are beautifully expressed in the lush lisianthus, the focus flower in this arrangement. Signifying "abundance," lisianthus is sometimes mistaken for a garden rose, but it is, in fact, the single layer of petals that allows the beholder to see abundance in the flower's simplicity. The addition of "virtue" brings depth to both the meaning and structure of the arrangement by adding texture with clary sage's vertical blooms and the fact that virtue's high moral standards add strength of character to the bouquet. Silver dollar eucalyptus adds an element of "protection," allowing the recipient of the flowers to feel abundantly safe, protected, and nurtured.

## Ingredients

**Appreciation:** ten stems blush lisianthus
**Esteem:** five stems salvia clary sage
**Protection:** five stems silver dollar eucalyptus

*Alternative botanicals:* alyssum, amethyst, angelica, bellflower/campanula, carnation, China aster, daffodil, dianthus, eucalyptus, fennel, fritillaria, heather, sage, salmonberry, spiderwort, St. John's wort, white geranium, yarrow

## To Create the Arrangement

1. Begin by filling a tall, narrow vessel three-quarters full of water.

2. Add a sphere of chicken wire to support the stems. If you don't have chicken wire, see additional plant support options on pages 25-26.

3. Place two stems of the drapiest silver dollar eucalyptus on each side of the vase to create a horizontal aspect.

4. Next cut two stems of lisianthus and place them to the side of the middle of the vase. Then add the other eight stems one by one, making sure that all the flowers are not at the same tall level.

5. To complete the arrangement, add an odd number of stems of clary sage to add color and texture.

6. If you have any gaps you would like to fill, tuck in some additional stems of eucalyptus and allow them to fall where they would like to.

> *Tip: Cluster the most eye-catching blooms in the lower center of an arrangement to anchor the arrangement.*

If I had a single
flower for every
time I think about
you, I could
walk forever
in my garden.

—Claudia
Adrienne Grandi

# BLISS

Let us be grateful to people who make us happy,
they are the charming gardeners who make our souls blossom.

*—Marcel Proust*

The combination of sweet pea's "blissful pleasure" and the hearty garden flower sweet William's "gallantry," along with the interesting juxtaposition of eucalyptus's "protection" (which adds the comfort of knowing one is safe) makes this the perfect bouquet to represent bliss. Create the arrangement to honor the blissful feeling that comes with finishing an important project, enjoying the pleasure of a lazy summer day, or the excitement of having done something outside of your comfort zone. As a gift, the bouquet will give someone you care about a symbolic pat on the back or simply invite some immensely fragrant bliss into a friend or loved one's cloudy day.

## Ingredients

**Blissful Pleasure:** fifteen stems sweet pea (mixed colors)

**Gallantry (dashing courage, heroic bravery):** seven stems sweet William

**Protection:** four stems silver dollar eucalyptus

*Alternative botanicals:* calendula, camellia, cosmos, larkspur, oregano, purple rose, rose of Sharon, salal, sweet sultan, tulip, white carnation, yellow lily

## To Create the Arrangement

1. This arrangement is created to be handheld but can be placed in water on a table or other natural shelf.

2. Before beginning, strip any lower leaves off the stems so they are easy to hold and work with.

3. Begin by holding multiple stems of sweet William gently in one hand. Gradually add in stems of sweet pea, allowing them to spread out and cascade down. If you have shorter stems, tuck them into the middle so the sweet William doesn't look too clumped together.

4. Turn the arrangement in your hand while continuing to add stems, allowing the blooms to spread out at the top so the arrangement is full yet airy.

5. To finish building the arrangement, tuck two to three silver dollar eucalyptus into the bouquet, allowing them to extend beyond the other blooms, which will keep the shape organic, giving the bouquet a natural and loose appearance.

6. Secure the bottom with twine.

*Tip: Arrange blooms so that they draw the eye up and out (or down and out) for dramatic and diagonal interest.*

The rose looks fair,
but fairer we it deem

For that sweet odour
which doth in it live.

—William Shakespeare

# BRAVERY

By the rivers of Babylon we sat down and wept

When we remembered Zion.

There the willow-trees

We hung our harps.

*—Psalm 137, The Bible*

Sometimes people we care about need extra encouragement to be boldly brave. Whether they are struggling with an ailment, getting through an emotionally difficult time, or taking on a physical feat that requires an extra serving of plucky audacity, a gorgeous dose of encouragement is exactly what is needed. Help dear ones courageously and victoriously conquer what is in front of them. The daring, spirited peony—meaning "bravery"—provides a stunning show of strength to get the job done, while the dusty-pink mauve roses provide grace under pressure. If you can't find willow branches, add a green vine, grass, or herbs for more color, contrast, and texture.

## Ingredients

**Bravery:** fifteen stems light pink peony
**Bravery:** six stems willow branches
**Grace:** six stems dusty-pink mauve rose

*Alternative botanicals:* black poplar, borage, cedar branches, edelweiss, fennel, ginger, gladiola, hollyhock, mullein, nasturtium, oak, protea, purple echinacea, red or burgundy astrantia, succulent, sweet William, yarrow

## To Create the Arrangement

1. For this arrangement choose a vessel that is not clear. Wind a few branches of willow (or the green vine if you cannot source willow) into a ball and place it in the vase before you add water. Be sure that the ball is low enough that the branches or vines don't stick out of the top. Then, fill the vase three-quarters full of water.

2. Next add the peonies stem by stem, placing some of the blooms that are the most closed in front so that they don't get hidden.

3. Look at the roses and note their different hues if they vary and then, one by one, intersperse them amongst the peonies, making sure to cluster similar shades of the roses together to keep the arrangement organic looking.

4. Finally, trim the willow branches (because they are naturally quite long) so that they extend approximately three to five inches above the other florals to give the bouquet a sense of natural movement and texture.

> *Tip:* Flexible branches not only make gorgeous points of interest in your arrangement but can also act as your mechanics, holding the other botanicals in place when balled up and secured in your vessel.

We are slumberous poppies
Lords of Lethe downs,
Some awake, and some asleep
Sleeping in our crowns.
What perchance our
dreams may know,
Let our serious beauty show.

—*William Shakespeare*

# CELEBRATION

Moreover, through the dancing poppies stole

A breeze, most softly lalling to my soul;

And shaping visions all about my sight

Of colours, wings, and burste of spangly light;

*—John Keats*

Times of joyful celebration are one of life's true pleasures. The combination of the exuberant peach and pink poppies—"fantastic extravagance"—and elegant white and purple cosmos—"joy in love and life"—makes this a vibrant bouquet that will encourage the recipient to celebrate. Create it for a job well done, to recognize an important achievement, or even to say, "Happy birthday." The geranium's meaningful "friendship" is tucked in to remind us that celebrations are even more satisfying when shared with those we love.

## Ingredients

**Fantastic Extravagance:** five stems poppy,
  mixed colors and sizes
**Joy in Love and Life:** ten stems cosmos,
  mixed colors
**Friendship:** three stems geranium leaves

*Alternative botanicals:* calendula, cape jasmine,
  celandine, dill, fennel, larkspur, laurel, lemon,
  lemon blossom, myrrh, nasturtium, oregano,
  sweet pea, tulip, wood sorrel

## To Create the Arrangement

1. For this arrangement, the blooms can simply be gradually gathered in one hand.

2. As stems are added, rotate the bouquet so that all sides will have blooms facing outward and upward.

3. Once you have created the size you want, stop adding blooms and surround the base with geranium leaves.

4. If you would like to keep it as a handheld arrangement, secure with ribbons (see page 44), or, if you prefer to put it in water, place the arrangement in a vase with a small mouth so it holds its shape.

*Tip: Poppies will last longer if you scorch the ends of the stems by quickly passing them through an open flame.*

Geoponika, the goddess…throwing herself in a hurry on the rose…was wounded by the thorns…and the rose, which was before white…became red and sweet-scented.

—*Ovid*

# CHARM

I cultivate a white rose

In July as in January

For the sincere friend

Who gives me his hand frankly.

And for the cruel person who tears out

the heart with which I Live,

I cultivate neither nettles nor thorns:

I cultivate a white rose.

*—Jose Marti*

Charm means "the power of pleasing or attracting," which makes this bouquet the perfect gift for someone who has captivated you or create it for yourself to invite some charm into your life. The magnetic combination of characteristics found in the cream spray roses, the musk spray roses, and the pink ranunculus are entwined here in the meanings "worthiness," "charm," and "radiant with charm." The antique white carnations are added to exhibit the lovely feeling that comes with being charmed while the "kindness" and "protection" found in the oats and eucalyptus add an element of depth and complexity to the sentiment.

## Ingredients

**Worthiness:** three stems white majolica cream spray rose

**Charm:** four stems musk cluster spray rose

**Radiant with Charm:** five stems pink ranunculus

**Loveliness, Sweetness:** four stems antique white carnation

**Kindness:** three stems oat

**Protection:** two stems gunni eucalyptus

*Alternative botanicals:* camellia, charmelia, eryngium/sea holly, flax, lily of the Nile, lisianthus, orange blossom, purple rose, sweet pea, succulent, white hyacinth, white jasmine, white lily

## To Create the Arrangement

1. Choose a bottom-heavy vessel and add strips of clear tape across the top in a grid pattern to support the flowers, because this arrangement has a strong horizontal component requiring stability for the stems.

2. If you have a watering can with a slim neck, add the water by placing the neck between the strips of tape so that the water doesn't get the vase wet where the tape is secured.

3. Begin by adding the gunni eucalyptus to create a base to the outside of the vase on the left and the right sides of the arrangement (angle the stems as much as possible so they droop).

4. Next, add the musk cluster spray roses, one stem at a time to act as a visual filler.

5. Add pops of color in the form of the pink ranunculus and position them low in the front. You may need to significantly cut the stems to achieve this look.

6. Finally, add the antique white roses with the blooms high up in the arrangement to create dimension.

7. Tuck in stems of oat, allowing them to peek out, adding texture and visual interest.

*Tip: Always cut carnations just above one of the nodes (bumps on the stalk) to give them an easier opportunity to absorb water.*

In a world of grief
and pain, flowers
bloom—even then.

—Kobayashi Issa

# COMFORT

Let us live like flowers; wild and beautiful and drenched in sun.

—*Ellen Everett*

Giving comfort and sympathy to others requires subtlety and quiet reassurance, all which are combined in this flower arrangement created to ease the mind and cheer the soul. Dahlias, meaning "dignity," are included in abundance to remind us that there is dignity even during times of distress. Necessary "comfort," symbolized by bee balm and scarlet geranium leaves, meaning "sympathy," are included to lend compassion. Strawflower and vintage white, silvery roses, both meaning "everlasting," are tucked in to remind us that even during difficult times, the everlasting presence of friends and family can be counted upon to lend support.

## Ingredients

**Dignity:** six stems Small World mini white pompon dahlia, three stems Linda's Baby dahlia

**Comfort:** five stems scarlet geranium leaves

**Sympathy:** seven stems bee balm (wild bergamot)

**Everlasting:** seven stems vintage white, silvery rose, and candy pink strawflower

Alternative botanicals: calendula, chamomile, elder, feverfew, hydrangea, Iceland moss, lemon balm, lily of the valley, oat, pear, pink rose, purple echinacea, thrift, white geranium, yarrow, yellow jasmine

## To Create the Arrangement

1. This simple handheld arrangement can be constructed in one hand while gradually adding in blooms with the other. Be sure to remove any thorns from the rose stems before handling them.

2. Begin by placing stems of the largest blooms in your hand (in this case the dahlias) and then do a quarter turn.

3. Next add in the roses and palm dahlias one stem at a time, continuing to turn the arrangement as you add in stems so blooms are facing in all directions.

4. Next add texture and color by including the pink strawflower and bee balm.

5. Once the bouquet is the desired size, add geranium around the bottom of the arrangement to create a lovely base.

6. Secure with twine, ribbon, or market wrap the arrangement once you have finished.

> *Tip:* Cut dahlia stems bleed proteins, sugars, and minerals that increase the likelihood of bacteria buildup, which, in turn, causes the bloom's life to rapidly decline. Combat this by changing the water and swapping or washing the vase daily. Also, if the dahlia blooms are beginning to wilt, place the stems in hot water and cool to room temperature for over an hour. This helps extend the life of the bloom(s) for another day or two.

Here's flowers for you;

Hot lavender, mints,
savoury, marjoram;

The marigold, that goes to
bed wi' the sun.

—*William Shakespeare*

# DEVOTION

And still she slept an azure-lidded sleep,

In blanched linen, smooth, and lavender'd,

While he from forth the closet brought a heap

Of candied apple, quince, and plum, and gourd;

With jellies soother than the creamy curd,

— *John Keats*

The trinity of flora signifying "devotion" in lavender, alstroemeria, and heliotrope bring strength to this bouquet. Whether one is assembling these blooms to show devotion to a special person or is creating this arrangement to reinforce a decision to devote one's energy to a particular outcome, these botanicals are the perfect focus. "Fidelity" in the form of veronica blooms, ornamental kale to signify "faithfulness," and gomphrena, signifying "unchangeable," show the nature of devotion's long-lasting character. Tucking in the succulent to show "tenacity" gives the bouquet the grit needed when the going sometimes gets rough because devotion can often require strength to keep going through thick and thin, no matter what hurdles are thrown across one's path.

## Ingredients

**Devotion:** one bunch English lavender, divided
**Devotion:** five stems pink and white alstroemeria
**Devotion:** five stems dark purple heliotrope
**Fidelity:** ten stems white veronica
**Unchangeable:** seven stems raspberry cream
gomphrena (globe amaranth)
**Faithfulness:** three stems ornamental
kale (crane)

**Tenacity:** one echeveria lilacina succulent
**Comfort:** five stems geranium leaves

*Alternative botanicals:* alyssum, astilbe,
baby's breath, blue violet, cedar, eucalyptus,
forget-me-not, honeysuckle, ivy, nasturtium,
passionflower, plum, sage, snowberry,
strawberry, strawflower

## To Create the Arrangement

1.  For this unique arrangement, place a double layer (one inside the other) of plastic grocery bags in a basket. Roll the outside of the bags together and then fill the bag three-quarters full of water while the basket is over the sink (if it leaks, you will know right away). Be sure to leave a couple of inches of bag at the top so water doesn't slosh out while the arrangement is transferred to where you will display it.

2.  Begin by adding the geranium and the ornamental kale (crane) to create a layer of filling. Place the kale at different locations in the arrangement, rather than in the middle, to give the arrangement an organic, natural feel.

3.  Add pops of color by inserting lavender in small clumps, veronica, and pink and white alstroemeria. Trim the stems to various heights and remove the lower leaves and greenery. Leave a few stems tall and place them at the back of the arrangement.

4.  Small clusters of dark purple heliotrope are added to the front of the arrangements—also at varying heights—and finish with raspberry cream gomphrena (globe amaranth).

5.  To add the succulent, remove as much dirt as possible. Wet the roots before adding to the arrangements if the roots won't reach the water. (This won't be a problem because the succulent will outlast the other blooms in the arrangement before beginning to wilt.) Position it off to one side.

> *Tip: When adding blooms with naturally short stems, double-check that they reach your water and adjust placement or water level accordingly.*

Yet mark'd I where the bolt of Cupid fell:

It fell upon a little western flower,

Before milk-white, now purple with
love's wound,

And maidens call it love-in-idleness.

— *William Shakespeare*

# ENCHANTMENT

Anna was not in lilac, as Kitty had so urgently wished, but in a black, low-cut, velvet gown, showing her full throat and shoulders, that looked as though carved in old ivory, and her rounded arms, with tiny, slender wrists. The whole gown was trimmed with Venetian guipure. On her head, among her black hair—her own, with no false additions—was a little wreath of pansies, and a bouquet of the same in the black ribbon of her sash among white lace.

—*Leo Tolstoy*

To be enchanted, enthralled, entranced is to be held spellbound by another, and this arrangement can be given to the special person whom you find enchanting or in support of a friend who would like to enchant someone in his or her life. At the heart of this arrangement is the "enchantment" of the lavender roses paired with the intentionality of pansies and violas, Victorian era favorites meaning "think of me" that were often exchanged by lovers to express longing. The columbine, meaning "resolve to win," gives the arrangement the intentionality of winning over the one who enchants. The clematis vine has been added to the arrangement to express the enchantment that comes from understanding like minds, while the ranunculus acknowledge the power of attraction. Finally, air plants are added to show that enchantment can be expressed freely and creatively.

## Ingredients

**Enchantment:** six stems lavender veil cabbage spray rose

**Resolve to Win:** five stems purple caerulea columbine and one bunch purple atrata columbine, divided

**Mental Beauty:** one blossom purple clematis on vine

**Think of Me:** eight stems purple pansy and viola

**Rich in Attractions:** eight stems purple ranunculus

**Freedom and Creativity:** three air plants

*Alternative botanicals:* cosmos, delphinium, dill, dwarf sunflower, eryngium/sea holly, fern, heliotrope, Lily of the Nile, lisianthus, musk cluster rose, orange rose, oregano, Queen Ann's lace, sweet pea, sweet sultan, white jasmine

## To Create the Arrangement

1. For this arrangement, place small jam jars and small-mouthed, single-stem vases within a container (because this arrangement uses jars and vases within the container, it's okay if the container is not watertight). Make sure the tops of the jars and small vases are not higher than the top of the container.

2. Fill the jars and vases three-quarters full of water.

3. To create a wild and whimsical look, begin by adding roses and ranunculus that are heavily reflexed (see page 30). Cut the stems so the flowers will be short and face them toward the front in the center. Begin with the shortest stems in the middle and then go outward, jar by jar, adding height so that the ranunculus are in an inverted bell curve.

4. Next, add the purple caerulea columbine and purple atrata columbine toward each side to add to the whimsicality and sense of enchantment.

5. Insert air plants as fillers along with a mixture of pansies and violas.

6. To finish the arrangement, reinforce (see page 27) a stem of clematis with a wooden skewer (a wooden chopstick or even a natural stick would also work) and then tuck it in at the front, toward the right.

> *Tip: When working with several different styles of blooms in one arrangement, choose one color and then let the variations of shades, sizes, and textures add chemistry. Also, if your roses are more closed than you want, try reflexing the bottom two layers of petals as described in the "Toolbox" section under "Reflexing Blooms."*

As Apollo is playing at quoits with the youth Hyacinthus, one of them, thrown by the Divinity, rebounds from the earth, and striking Hyacinthus on the head, kills him. From his blood springs up the flower which still bears his name.

—*Ovid*

# FORGIVENESS

You gave me hyacinths first a year ago; They called me the hyacinth girl.'

—Yet when we came back, late, from the Hyacinth garden,

Your arms full, and your hair wet, I could not

Speak, and my eyes failed, I was neither Living nor dead, and I knew nothing,

Looking into the heart of light, the silence.

*—T.S. Eliot*

If you need to ask someone for forgiveness or open yourself to forgiving a hurt done to you, this delicate arrangement holds the ingredients you need. The focus flower for "forgiveness," purple hyacinth, expresses mercy and pardon. The single bulb in each pot emphasizes the reality that sometimes asking forgiveness (or granting it) is a simple-yet-powerful act. The complex petals that make up the hyacinth's flower structure show that the intricacies of compassion and mercy ultimately lead to reconciliation.

## Ingredients

**Forgiveness:** one bulb purple hyacinth

*Alternative botanicals:* almond blossom, bachelor button/cornflower, blue scilia, bluebell, broom, China aster, Christmas rose, cranberry, elder, hawthorn, hazel, hellebore, hyssop, iris, mistletoe, nemophelia/baby blue eyes, pink rose, pink astrantia, red carnation, spruce, snowdrop, thrift, wisteria, yarrow

## To Create the Arrangement

1. Sometimes simple is perfect, and in this case, creating an arrangement with planted bulbs of hyacinth is all that's needed. The fact that the top of the bulb is peeking out is a visual reminder of the deep-rootedness of the need for forgiveness.

> *Tip: Perennial bulbs in bloom make beautiful standalone gifts that also stand the test of time, reblooming year and year for your recipient to enjoy. No filler or flutter needed. Sometimes less is more.*

Give me odorous
at sunrise a garden
of beautiful flowers,
where I can walk undisturbed…

—Walt Whitman

# FRIENDSHIP

*A flower does not think of competing with the flower next to it. It just blooms.*

*—Zen Chin*

Our friends anchor us in life. The deep, lasting bonds of friendship are expressed with freesias because their long-lasting blooms are reminders that our friends are there for us through good times and bad. Mint's "virtue" and lemon balm's "sympathy" are both qualities of true friendship and oak leaf geranium is included for its pure meaning of "friendship." This bouquet is the perfect gift to give your friends for any or no occasion because it's always nice to show your friends how truly appreciated they are.

## Ingredients

**Lasting Friendship:** five stems white freesia
**Virtue:** five sprigs mint
**Luck and Love to Women:** five sprigs
 lemon balm
**Friendship:** two stems oak leaf geranium

*Alternative botanicals:* alyssum, angelica, blue periwinkle, calendula, China aster, clematis, dianthus, elder, fennel, flax, fritillaria, ivy, lavender, lisianthus, oat, orchid, nasturtium, peppermint, salmonberry, strawflower, thrift, wax flower, white jasmine, zinnia

## To Create the Arrangement

1. Begin by gathering the mint and catmint and create a small simple handheld nosegay.

2. Tuck in geranium leaves for filler.

3. Finally nestle white freesia into the bouquet not only to add blooms but also to symbolize the closeness of lasting friendship. Make sure the blooms are just above the herbs so they are a lovely focal point.

4. Secure the stems with a ribbon to create a simple-yet-perfect gift.

5. If inviting your friend over, adorn the table with pansies (meaning "think of me," along with eggs, commonly symbolizing hope, purity, femininity, and fertility) to add extra layers of meaning.

> *Tip: Herbs are an excellent foliage choice for bouquets, often acting as filler, foliage, flutter, and fragrance all in one stem!*

And the goddess answered my question thus, and while she spoke, her lips breathed vernal roses: "I who now am called Flora was formerly Chloris."

—Ovid

# GRACE

Around them bloomed the roses with a mad, amorous blossoming,
full of crimson and rosy and white laughter.

—*Emile Zola*

The word *grace* brings to mind images of subtle beauty, a refined sense of elegance, and bountiful forgiveness. This arrangement symbolizes the various facets of this powerful word. Pink roses, meaning "grace," are the centerpiece with antique cream stock interspersed to express the lasting beauty of true grace. Sword ferns are added to express the sincerity of the emotion and grapes are draped over the edge to symbolize the abundant gratitude, gladness, and joy we find when enveloped in the beauty and poise of grace.

## Ingredients

**Grace:** five stems pink cottage rose, one cluster white geranium
**Lasting Beauty:** six stems antique cream stock
**Sincerity:** three stems Western sword fern
**Abundance:** one bunch champagne grapes

*Alternative botanicals:* bluebell, broom, calla lily, clove, dahlia, elm, garden chervil, honesty, magnolia, peach rose, pink astrantia, yellow jasmine, viola, white geranium

## To Create the Arrangement

1. For this arrangement, choose a cylindrical vessel, place a flower frog (see page 25) at the bottom, anchor it with floral putty, and then fill the vase three-quarters full of water.

2. Begin by securing the stems of roses into the flower frog so they can be in an upright position but angling outward.

3. Next, add the stems of stock to fill in the arrangement.

4. Tuck fern at the bottom of the arrangement (they don't have to reach the flower frog) to add texture.

5. Create a false stem (see page 28) and then adhere it to the base of the grapes. Place it in the front of the arrangement so the grapes will cascade down the vessel.

> *Tip: The outermost layer of petals on any rose are called the guard petals. Leave them intact until you are ready to incorporate them into your arrangement, as removing them signals the flower to start opening.*

> *Tip: If your roses are more closed than you want, try reflexing the bottom two layers of petals as described in the "Toolbox" section under "Reflexing Blooms."*

To live, one must have sunshine, freedom, and a little flower!

—Hans Christian Andersen

The Love Language of Flowers

# HAPPINESS

Perfumes are the feelings of flowers, and as the human heart, imagining itself alone and unwatched, feels most deeply in the night-time, so seems it as if the flowers, in musing modesty, await the mantling eventide ere they give themselves up wholly to feeling, and breathe forth their sweetest odours. Flow forth, ye perfumes of my heart, and seek beyond these mountains the dear one of my dreams!

—*Heinrich Heine*

Delphinium's lighthearted happiness and Gerbera daisy's "cheerfulness" combine to create a meaning perfectly suited for this bouquet. The vibrant delphinium stems can either be left tall and placed in large vessels to make a grand statement, cut down to create nosegays to adorn the table at a dinner party or tucked into bud vases and grouped for drama. Oregano's "joy in love and life" adds additional color and texture and acknowledges that sharing happy times with loved ones brings a sense of fullness to life. Any of these bouquets symbolizing happiness makes a perfect hostess gift, housewarming present, or offering for anyone you wish the blessing of happiness.

## Ingredients

**Cheerful:** eleven stems hot pink Gerbera daisy, stems Bokito pomponi Gerbera daisy

**Levity and Happiness:** four stems hybrid purple delphinium

**Joy in Love and Life, Soothing, Banish Sadness:** seven stems of Kent Beauty oregano clusters.

*Alternative botanicals:* calendula, China aster, coreopsis, cosmos, dill, lily of the valley, mugwort, myrrh, poinsettia, salal, spring crocus, sweet pea, sweet sultan, tulip, yellow lily

## To Create the Arrangement

Before you begin, gather five small vases of varying sizes and heights that have a cohesive aesthetic. Gather the botanicals to be used to create these five unique arrangements.

> *Tip: When choosing a vessel, consider the size of the mouth opening. Large mouths will allow you to position your blooms on striking angles, adding horizontal interest, while small, mouthed vessels will force stems to stand upright at attention.*

### Focus Arrangement

1. First create the arrangement in the largest vase because it will be the one with the most flowers in the composition. This is the focus arrangement.

2. To begin, add a small frog to the vase because the delphinium and daisy will need support. Anchor it with floral putty. Then fill the vase three-quarters with water.

3. Strip the stem of the delphinium halfway up and trim the stems to slightly different heights. Place them into the vase, positioned toward the back.

4. In front of those, place the daisies at varying heights and do the same with the Bokito pomponi.

5. To finish, tuck the oregano around the bottom, and, if possible, secure the stems into the flower frog because this variety of oregano is top-heavy. Allow it to drape down the side of the vase to add drama.

## Second Arrangement

+ Fill the vase three-quarters of water and trim the stems of the florals to varying lengths. Add one delphinium, one sprig of oregano, and one stem of daisy to add visual drama.

## Third Arrangement

1. This arrangement is a testimony to the power of threes in flower arranging (or for larger arrangements use odd numbers)

2. Add one spring of oregano.

3. Next add three daisies as the focal flower to show that being amongst friends adds cheer to one's life.

## Fourth Arrangement

+ This single bloom, alone, shows that one can find cheer in even the most simple, lovely things in life.

## Fifth Arrangement

+ The fifth arrangement features gorgeous oregano foliage. Foliage is often overlooked in arrangements, but it can be a beautiful focal point.

A flower blossoms for
its own joy.

—*Oscar Wilde*

# JOY

When amang the crisp heather upon the hill-side,

Mine e'e fu' o' rapture, my soul fu' o' pride;

The wee heather-untie an' wild hinny-bee

A' join in the strain wi' my fiddle an' me.

—*James Ballentine*

When tulips were first introduced to Europe in the 1600s, a fervor swept the world henceforth known as *Tulipmania*. These vivacious flowers have inspired joy and passion ever since. Tulip meanings subtly change depending on their color, but all fall into the positive spectrum of "love" and "joy" in one form or another. These lively blossoms can be given to friends, lovers, someone you suspect could be a special person in your life, in celebration of an event, or even as encouragement to someone who needs some joy and love. The addition of white jasmine's uplifting "amiability" adds texture and gracefulness as well as a gorgeous scent and feverfew's "warmth" brings depth to the sense of joy. Note: In this arrangement, jasmine vines were used because flowering jasmine was not in season when it was created. Either flowering or unflowering is fine to use.

## Ingredients

**Joy and Declaration of Love:** seven stems white tulip

**Amiability:** nine stems white jasmine foliage

**Warmth:** five small clusters feverfew

*Alternative botanicals:* calendula, coreopsis, cosmos, delphinium, Gerbera daisy, oregano, poinsettia, sweet sultan, yellow lily

## To Create the Arrangement

1. For this arrangement, begin with a shallow vessel or bowl and then wind the jasmine vines into a circle roughly the same dimensions as the vessel. When the end of the vine reached, simply tuck it in. Then place the ball of jasmine vines into the vessel. Repeat the process two more times and tuck them into the vessel. It's okay if it pops out of the top.

2. Tuck a flower frog (in this case, it is a cage frog, but any frog will do) into the middle of the vine twists and then fill water to approximately three-quarters full.

3. Snip additional stems of jasmine and add them to the frog, sticking out toward the sides and back. Allow them to droop if that's what they naturally do.

4.  Next add in the tulips, stem by stem, beginning with the shortest one in the middle and then one longer stem to the left and another long one to the right. Gently tease the stems into a curve on the right side so they will be uneven and organic-looking. Repeat the same with a second stem on the right. Add additional straight stems into the middle and then add more tall stems on the left. After the tulips are in position, bend the leaves of three of them down to add a sense of whimsy.

5.  Finish by adding feverfew in small clusters of approximately six to eight stems and place them in the frog, low enough for the stems to reach the water. If you prefer to hide the frog, mound the feverfew in front of it so it is no longer visible. Or, if you have an antique frog that you would like to remain visible, add fewer stems so that it shows through.

*Tip: Tulips should be closed when harvested or purchased, with only a hint of color showing. When creating your arrangement, keep in mind that, as your tulips rest overnight, tulip stems will loosen from their rigid stance to a graceful, beautiful, curving bend.*

*Tip: Tulips are phototropic, meaning they grow toward the nearest light source. Keep this in mind when choosing where your tulip arrangements will be displayed.*

The Love Language of Flowers

Each flower on bells of
Ireland brings a wish your
way: good health, good
luck, and happiness for
today and every day.

—*Irish Proverb*

# LUCK

Her lawn looks like a meadow
And if she mows the place
She leaves the clover standing
And the Queen Anne's Lace.

—*Edna St. Vincent Millay*

The Irish are known for their luck, so it is only appropriate that the flower symbolizing good fortune is as lushly green as the Emerald Isle. Wishing others well in an endeavor is a privilege that comes with love and friendship, so this arrangement is best presented in a basket ready to gift. Queen Anne's lace, the delicate flower symbolizing "fantasy," is included because one element of good luck is the dream—or fantasy—of blissful success. Pom pom ranunculus bring a sense of charm because those with luck lead a charmed life.

## Ingredients

**Luck:** five stems bells of Ireland
**Fantasy:** six stems chocolate Queen Anne's lace
**Radiant with Charm:** ten stems green and
white pom pom ranunculus

*Alternative botanicals:* camellia, China aster,
musk cluster rose, sweet basil, white jasmine

## To Create the Arrangement

1. For this arrangement, a small, handheld gathering basket was used, but any basket will do. Place two wide-mouth mason-style jars, carryout containers, or other watertight containers. Fill them three-quarters full of water. If your basket doesn't sit on its own, support it between books or other sturdy objects that will allow it to remain upright.

2. Often the foliage at the top of belles of Ireland is removed, but in this arrangement the foliage was kept on and used as filler. Cut the stems so they are not too tall and remove the blooms from the bottom so the stem is clean where it enters the water.

3. Next add Queen Anne's lace as a filler throughout the arrangement, giving it more of a mounded look to mirror the curve of the bottom of the basket. Allow them to fall forward and to the side to give the arrangement the look of foraged flowers.

4. Finish by tucking in the stems of ranunculus to add pops of color.

*Tip: When adding bold-colored blooms to a base of green foliage, sporadically integrate them so that the spacing is not overly symmetrical. Position some blooms clustered or closer together, others farther apart, and none in a straight line.*

"Look at us," said the violets,
blooming at her feet. "All last
winter we slept…but here we
are to comfort you."

—Edward Payson Roe

# MATERNAL LOVE

But they claimed that they had neither seen nor heard the baby, born four days ago. For it had been hidden in the rushes and the boundless thicket, his tender body washed in the golden and purple light of violets.

*—Pindar*

A mother's love surrounds her child. It's steadfast and faithful. In this arrangement, maternal love, symbolized by the moss's warm, blanketing structure surrounds a violet meaning "faithfulness" or "worth" because what is more worthy of love than a child? Purple in particular means "filled with love," making this the perfect arrangement to celebrate the purity of a mother's unconditional love.

## Ingredients

**Maternal Love:** moss to cover soil

**Faithfulness, Worth, or Filled with Love:** one
  African violet plant

*Alternative botanicals:* alstroemeria, baby's
  breath, bluebell, blue hyacinth, blue violet,
  cedar, eucalyptus, geranium, globe amaranth/
  gomphrena, heather, heliotrope, honeysuckle,
  lavender, ornamental kale/crane, pink rose,
  St. John's wort, strawflower, white geranium,
  wood sorrel, yarrow

## To Create the Arrangement

1.  If giving this arrangement to the mom in your life, make the vessel a meaningful gift. In this
    case a handmade coffee mug was used to create this arrangement.

2.  Transplant the African violet into the mug, adding additional soil if needed, and tuck moss
    around the edges. Alternatively, the plant can be placed in the mug without removing the
    planter so it can be easily removed.

> *Tip:* African violets prefer to be watered from the bottom up, as their leaves resent
> being wet. Place your pot in a tray of shallow water for thirty minutes to allow the soil
> to soak up the water through its drainage holes. Also, moss is an excellent botanical to
> incorporate when you wish to hide mechanics or soil and can often be foraged.

I meant to do my work today
But a brown bird sang in the apple tree
And a butterfly flitted across the field
And all the leaves were calling me.

—*Richard le Gallienne*

# MISS YOU

I belong to you like this plot of land

That I planted with flowers

And sweet-smelling herbs.

Sweet in its stream

Shy by your hand

Refreshing in the north wind.

A lovely place to wander in

Your hand in my hand.

—Ruth Binney

If you are pining for that certain someone, need to reconcile with an important person in your life, or simply want to put form to feelings of longing, this combination of flower meanings entwines to create an arrangement to express your sentiment. The focus flowers, zinnias, mean both "thoughts of you" and "I mourn your absence" while the stems of astrantia are included to bolster strength and courage to get through the feeling of loss. The fact that we miss those whom we prefer over others is represented by the addition of beautiful apple branches ripe with fruit.

## Ingredients

**Thoughts of You/I Mourn Your Absence:**
seven Queen Red Lime zinnias, varying sizes

**Preference:** three apple tree branches with
hanging fruit

**Strength, Courage:** five stems
burgundy astrantia

*Alternative botanicals:* astilbe, bee balm,
calendula, cape jasmine, celandine,
chamomile, China aster, forsythia, Japanese
anemone, pear, red carnation, scarlet
geranium, white periwinkle, wisteria,
wood sorrel

## To Create the Arrangement

1. Anchor a hairpin frog, using floral putty, into a ceramic vase and then fill three-quarters
   with water.

2. Trim the apple branches to a length that allows the fruit to hang or rest toward the bottom of
   the arrangement and then insert the two branches into the frog, allowing one to lean to the
   right and one to the left. Because the fruit is heavy, it is important to insert the stems securely
   into the frog so the arrangement is well supported. Allow them to lean on the edge of the
   vase for additional support.

3. Add the zinnias, stem by stem, as the focus flower. Begin by placing one low in the front
   toward the left and a second one high and then for the remaining stems, intersperse them in a
   visually pleasing way.

4. Next add in the burgundy astrantia in small clusters: one of them tall to add a sense of flutter and the others lower to hide the top of the vessel. Tuck in a few medium-length astrantia around the fruit to secure the arrangement.

5. Cut an additional apple branch down to the first set of apples and then add stem length by wrapping floral tape around the stem and a skewer. Clip or snap the skewer to the length that will allow the apple to be at a higher level than the first two branches. If some apples fall off the branches, they can still be included by placing them on wooden skewers and adding them to the arrangement.

6. To finish the arrangement with a sense of whimsy, tuck in one additional cluster of astrantia above the skewered apples so they are visually incorporated into the bouquet.

*Tip: When adding fruit, search for fruit that is currently in season and position a cluster off-center in your arrangement. Add balance by positioning a single piece (or smaller cluster) in a different location diagonal to the first.*

The heart of a mother
is a deep abyss at the
bottom of which
you will always
find forgiveness.

—Honore de Balzac

# MOTHER'S DAY BOUQUET

When daffodils begin to peer,

With heigh! the doxy over the dale,

Why, then comes in the sweet o' the year;

—*William Shakespeare*

Motherhood is one of the most complex and beautiful aspects of many women's lives and this bouquet pulls in a mixture of the many emotions evoked while being a mom. It begins with "joy, perfect love and a declaration of love" when mothers first lay eyes on their children, which is introduced with apricot parrot tulips. "Grace" of course, is needed to get through the times that mothers are tested, but no matter what their children put them through, there is always "purity" and "hope," which are represented by the perfect white summer snowflake Leucojum. "Protection" in the form of gunni eucalyptus, is every mother's top priority. The fact that mothers and children find each other beautiful inside and out is represented with cream stock. Finally, salix, also known as French pussy willow, is included because the meaning is "motherhood" and is truly fitting because it is not only strong but soft.

## Ingredients

**Grace:** six stems pink rose

**Joy, Perfect Love, Declaration of Love:** ten stems apricot parrot tulips, orange fringe tulips, and Verona sunrise tulips.

**Admiration, Regard:** three stems fragrant Cheerfulness daffodil

**Purity, Hope:** three stems white Leucojum/ summer snowflake

**Lasting Beauty, You Will Always Be Beautiful to Me:** five stems cream stock

**Protection:** four stems gunni eucalyptus

**Motherhood:** seven dried stems salix (French pussy willow)

*Alternative botanicals:* acacia (pink or white), alyssum, African violet, baby's breath, blue hyacinth, cedar, clematis, dwarf sunflower, geranium, globe amaranth/gomphrena, heliotrope, honeysuckle, lavender, lisianthus, moss, orchid, pin cushion/scabiosa, pink astrantia, pink dianthus, ranunculus, strawflower, succulent, thrift

## To Create the Arrangement

1. Like motherhood, this arrangement is complex and may take practice. Choose a bowl, a wide pitcher, or a vase with a wide opening.

2. Add a sphere of chicken wire to support the stems and then secure the chicken wire with clear tape. If you don't have chicken wire, see different plant support options on pages 25-26.

3. Begin by securing the gunni eucalyptus into the chicken wire at an angle to the sides and the back.

4. Intersperse the fringe tulips, pink Verona tulips, daffodils, and roses, adding them at varying lengths one stem at a time. Choose the biggest, most dramatic blooms to place lowest in front and slowly add the stems upward and outward.

5. Next, add the stock for additional fragrance and filler and then the white Leucojum/summer snowflake, making sure they pop out for whimsy—because they are delicate and can easily be lost in the arrangement.

6. Finally, add fresh or dried willow branches to add complexity and sophistication.

> *Tip:* When creating a traditional arrangement with a rounded shape, position your thickest, strongest stems to stand as the tallest, as they will maintain their structure longer than the thinner ones.

There was a rustle of chirruping sparrows in the green lacquer leaves of the ivy, and the blue cloud-shadows chased themselves across the grass like swallows. How pleasant it was in the garden! And how delightful other people's emotions were!— much more delightful than their ideas, it seemed to him.

—Oscar Wilde

# PASSIONATE LOVE

I begin to sing of ivy-crowned Dionysus, the loud-crying god, splendid son of Zeus and glorious Semele. The rich-haired Nymphs received him in their bosoms from the lord his father and fostered and nurtured him carefully in the dells of Nysa, where by the will of his father he grew up in a sweet-smelling cave, being reckoned among the immortals.

*—Homeric Hymn to Dionysus*

Whether it's passionate desire or yearning, emotions can be consuming, and passionate love is the most intense of all. The primary flower in this bouquet, red rose, focuses on romantic passion. The Sahara beige cabbage rose adds a layer of complexity because love is indeed multi-faceted. "Joy" and "perfect love" are introduced with purple tulips to express the blissful feeling of being in love. Devotion is added with the stems of pink veronica and vines of Algerian Ivy, both meaning "fidelity." Embrace the tiny imperfections in the roses, such as the dry tips of the petals, because even those we passionately adore are flawed and accepting imperfections in others is a powerful part of love.

## Ingredients

**Passionate Love:** seven red spray roses
**Love:** twelve stems Sahara beige cabbage rose
**Joy and Perfect Love:** eight stems purple tulip
**Fidelity:** seven stems pink veronica
**Fidelity, Wedded Love:** seven vines
 Algerian ivy

*Alternative botanicals:* azalea, bougainvillea, dianthus, heliotrope, juniper, mossy saxifrage, Niphetos rose, pear, Queen Ann's lace, red metamorph marigold, red or burgundy astrantia, rose of Sharon, salal, sorrel, Spanish jasmine, sweet pea, tuberose, white dittany, wisteria

## To Create the Arrangement

1. For this arrangement, a handled basket was used, but any flat-bottomed basket will work.

2. Place mason jars in the bottom of the basket so that the jars fit snugly together. Fill the jars three-quarters full of water. (Even if you don't use them all, keep the jars in the basket so they don't shift if you move the basket.)

3. Begin by placing stems of ivy in the jars located both in the front and off to one side so it looks like it is cascading down naturally. If the basket has a handle, twist one vine of ivy around it.

4. Next, add in the Sahara beige cabbage roses in a random pattern, gently reflexing them as they are added so that they, as the focal flower, are the larger, more open blooms.

5. Add the red spray roses, including a random number per jar, so it looks natural. Continue to add stems until all the gaps are filled.

6. If your basket has a handle, allow it to peek through.

7. Finally, add the veronica and tulips, poking out above the roses to add varying colors and textures. When selecting the stems of veronica, try to position the brightest blooms in the most prominent positions.

*Tip: When working with vines and lengthy stems, arrange them to act as they naturally would when growing. Vines should cling, crawl, wander, and dangle. Long, wild stems have a habit of stretching and curving out.*

Trees that
are slow
to grow
bear the
best fruit.

—Molière

# PATIENCE

Flowers and fruits are always fit presents; flowers because they are a proud assertion
that a ray of beauty outvalues all the utilities of the world…

*—Ralph Waldo Emerson*

When a sense of patience is required to get through a
trying moment or when watching the seemingly slow
passage of time while waiting for something
wonderful to happen, this simple arrangement is a
reminder that the desired moment will arrive.
"Patience" in the form of moonstone China aster,
placed in a series of individual vases and combined
with canary grass and bunny tail grass, is a reminder
that perseverance will pay off.

## Ingredients

**Patience:** fifteen stems moonstone China aster
**Perseverance:** one bunch canary grass, divided three stems bunny tail grass

*Alternative botanicals:* astilbe, dock, fuschia, holly, hydrangea, liatris, ox-eye daisy, pink astrantia, pink rose, strawberry, yellow jasmine

## To Create the Arrangement

1. When people think about bottle arrangements, clear glass is often chosen, but if you have a few colored glass bottles, jars, or vases, it will add drama and a color pop. They are especially beautiful outdoors because the sunlight shows through and adds a stunning impact.

2. Fill the bottles three-quarters full and position them so it is pleasing to your eye and fits the size of the table. If the table is round, cluster them in a circle with the tallest bottles in the center. For a rectangular table, create a straight line with the bottles, staggering the heights and widths as you go.

3. Begin by adding the moonstone China aster one stem at a time, placing the longest stems in the tallest bottles and then trimming the stems down for the shorter bottles. Vary the number of stems per bottle (either one flower or three flowers per vase) for a natural, organic look. Position the blooms so that they face different directions.

4. Tuck the grasses into the bottles to add an element of texture and flutter. You can even include grasses only in a bottle or two for variation.

5. For added drama, add a few blooms on the table beside the jars. Asters will remain beautiful and fresh-looking for many hours out of water.

*Tip: Dried botanicals are a great alternative to fresh when searching for an added element of texture or seasonal bling.*

The olive
branch of peace
is of use.

—*Ovid*

# PEACE

The mortal moon hath her eclipse endured
And the sad augurs mock their own presage;
Uncertainties now crown themselves assured
And peace proclaims olives of endless age.

— *William Shakespeare*

Olive branches have symbolized peace for thousands of years and this beautiful wreath is the quintessential peace offering. Give this wreath as a symbol of peace, simply for beauty's sake or hang it on a front door to show that your home is a place of tranquility and welcome for those entering. Historically evergreen wreaths have represented the forthcoming rebirth of spring when hung during the darkest days of winter. Peaceful olive branch wreaths can also be adorned with colorful berries, fruit, flowers, or other foliage to bring color, such as the snowberries tucked into the wreath to signify a sense of connectedness. Peppermint is another great inclusion for wreaths of this nature. Symbolizing friendship and warmth, this herb also yields a fresh scent as people are welcomed into your home.

## Ingredients

**Peace:** one bunch (about ten) olive branches plus fifteen to twenty small olive sprigs

**Bear Together and Connection:** one bunch snowberry, divided

**Friendship and Warmth:** one bunch peppermint, divided

One metal wreath base

*Alternative botanicals:* chamomile, hydrangea, lily of the valley, mugwort, pin cushion/scabiosa, poppy, sedum, stonecrop

## To Create the Arrangement

1.  Take the set of ten tall olive branches and attach them to the base by weaving them over and under the sections. Weave the bottom end of the branch in a counterclockwise motion, pulling it through as you weave until the end is on the base. Because the branches are fresh, they will be pliable and easy to weave. Be sure that your leaves are all facing the same direction in a clockwise position.

2. Attach the end of florist wire to the base with a simple knot or by winding it around the outermost wire ring of the base a few times. Do not cut it. Leave it connected to the roll and continue to unroll as you secure the branches.

3. Create fifteen to twenty mini bundles of botanicals, starting with five to seven olive branch sprigs as the base, and then cluster your herbs on top as a second layer. No need to secure them together; piles will do.

4. Fan out one of the botanical bundles and place it on the base, keeping the leaves pointed clockwise. Wrap the wire around the bottom of the bundle tightly three or four times where your thumb was holding them together. Do not cut the wire. Continue unwinding while wrapping and securing the bundles to the base in a spiral motion. (It's important to wind the wire around your bundles *very tightly,* as the botanicals will shrink as they dry.)

5. Attach the next bundle just above (or behind) the first one, layering the herbs so that the "fan" of the second bundle covers the wire you used to attach the first bundle. Continue this step until the entire wreath is filled. The number of bundles you need will vary, depending on how large and tall your bundles are, how much (or little) you overlap each bundle, and the size of your wreath base.

6. When you are about to attach the final herb bundle, tuck the base of the bundle underneath the fan of the first bundle you attached. This will complete the circle and ensure that all the florist wire is hidden by foliage. Then, give the wire a bit of a tail and cut it. Secure the tail to the back of the wreath, winding it tightly.

7. (Optional) Add dried botanicals or fresh berries by tucking them into the attached bundles, spacing them out around the wreath or clustering them in one area. Bows can be attached with a twelve-inch piece of florist wire.

*Tip: Don't feel obligated to fill the entire circumference of your wreath. Particularly if you are using natural branches as the wreath base, consider only filling two-thirds (primarily the left side and bottom) or the bottom third of the wreath and leaving the rest exposed. Also, to keep your wreath green and smelling lovely, mist it with water every day.*

And by the dusty road
Bedstraw and Mullein tall,
With red Valerian
And Toadflax on the wall,

Yarrow and Chicory,
That hath for hue no like,
Silene and Mallow mild
And Agrimony's spike.

—Robert Bridges

# PROTECTION

I will pluck the smooth yarrow that my figure may be sweeter,
that my lips may be warmer, that my voice may be gladder.

—*Traditional Gaelic Quote*

An interwoven sense of well-being in the form of botanical security is created with the compilation of these protective flora: heather, dried yellow yarrow, silver dollar eucalyptus, and St. John's wort buds—all which mean "protection"—are gathered to form a powerful shield that can be given or kept close at hand when a safe sanctuary is desired.

## Ingredients

**Protection:** five stems heather
**Protection:** five stems dried yellow yarrow
**Protection:** three stems silver dollar eucalyptus
**Protection:** three stems St. John's wort buds

*Alternative botanicals:* cedar, hellebore, white geranium

## To Create the Arrangement

1. Begin by choosing a tall vessel with a wide mouth. Anchor a floral frog with floral putty and then fill three-quarters of water.

2. Begin by adding the eucalyptus as the anchor flower. For this arrangement, it looks lovely whether it's upright or dipping down. To keep it upright, simply trim the stems and place them in the frog to keep them standing up or to let them droop, keep them longer.

3. Next add the heather, position four of the stems equally in the vase, and then trim the fifth stem shorter and place it in the front.

4. Add the yarrow, clustered in the lower front, to add a pop of color and texture.

5. To finish, add St. John's wort buds, trimmed down, to complete the meaning.

> *Tip: When considering colors, those on opposite sides of the color wheel often intensify and complement each other, making both colors seem more vibrant than when they stand alone.*

His heart beat faster as Daisy's white face came up to his own. He knew that when he kissed this girl, and forever wed his unutterable visions to her perishable breath, his mind would never romp again like the mind of God. So he waited, listening for a moment longer to the tuning-fork that had been struck upon a star. Then he kissed her.

—F. Scott Fitzgerald

# PURITY

'That is true indeed, by my own selfhood,'

Quoth Love, 'you have knowledge, I see,

If that is what you think, but now tell me,

Have you not read in a book, in your chest,

Of the great goodness of queen Alceste,

Who became the daisy, the day's eye;

She that for her husband chose to die,

And thus to go to Hell rather than he,

She who was rescued then by Hercules,

Who brought her out of Hell again to bliss?'

—Geoffrey Chaucer

If fortunate in life, there are a few people we love, plain and simple. Daisy's "innocence" and blush scabiosa's "purity and peace" express our pure love for those special people in our lives. The strawberry blossom's meaning of "perfection" doesn't imply that we must be perfect to be loved but that loving each other brings out the best versions of ourselves. Bracken and Western sword fern are included to add "sincerity" to the sentiment.

## Ingredients

**Innocence:** twenty-eight stems white daisy
**Perfection:** eight stems strawberry (with differing stages of fruit growth)
**Purity, Peace:** six stems blush scabiosa
**Sincerity:** five stems bracken and Western sword fern

*Alternative botanicals:* gardenia, hibiscus, hyssop, Leucojum/summer snowflake, orange blossom, orchid, pin cushion/scabiosa, star of Bethlehem, viola, white astrantia, white lilac, white lily, white sedum

## To Create the Arrangement

1. This arrangement puts clustering stems of what would often be filler together to create a dramatic focus.

2. Begin adding a pin frog to a mason jar, affixing it with floral putty. Then fill it three-quarters with water and trip the foliage off the bottom of the daisy stems where they will be in the water. Then place the daisies into the jar as they fall. Hold back approximately five stems of daisies and trim them shorter to add to the front.

3. Next add scabiosa, clustering three together at the top of the arrangement, and two in the middle and one down and off to the left to subtly add visual balance.

4. To add the strawberries, preferably add them trimmed from growing plants, but if that is not available for you, then skewer the strawberries onto sticks to create a false stem (see page 28).

5. To finish, trim the fern stems to varying lengths and then strip the foliage from the bottom half to leave an exposed stem. (If you leave the foliage on, it will quickly lead to bacteria buildup in the water, shortening the life of the arrangement.)

6. Keep the ferns in a cluster and place them into the jar on the left side to create not only focus but also drama.

*Tip: Cluster stems together to shine a spotlight on that botanical.*

I will be the gladdest thing
Under the sun!
I will touch a hundred flowers
And not pick one…
—Edna St. Vincent Millay

# REFINEMENT

The flowers have spoken to me more than I can tell in written words.
They are hieroglyphics of angels, loved for the beauty of their character,
though few can decipher even fragments of their meaning.

—*Lydia Maria Child*

Few flowers have the visual presence of the elegant gardenia, which means "refinement." Their minimalist sophistication makes them timeless. In small groupings, they add a chic sensibility to décor and their message of refined elegance makes them perfect lapel flowers or additions to bridal bouquets. The heady scent of gardenias belies the understatement of these luscious blossoms.

## Ingredients

**Refinement:** three gardenia blooms

*Alternative botanicals:* hyssop, orchid, strawberry, tulip

## To Create the Arrangement

1. The concept behind this display is to allow these delicate flowers to be a dramatic focal point.

2. Choose two short vessels, fill them three-quarters with water, and gently lay the gardenias on top.

3. For added drama, place a third blossom on an antique spoon or on the tabletop by the arrangement. If you have a delicate scarf, wrap it around the vessels.

> *Tip:* *The petals will turn brown wherever they are touched, so be careful not to touch any parts of the flower that will show in the arrangement. Also, gardenias are sensitive to high chlorine levels so float them in distilled water rather than tap water.*

It is not on the artist's canvas,
but in the gardener's flower that
the greatest wealth of color may
be seen… Flowers possess the next
best quality of color tone to that
which we see in the rainbow.

—F. Schuyler Mathews

# REMEMBRANCE

And I don't care that the day
with the night will be cloudy,
that with the light that emanated
his spirit would live.
For this true love
that bites my simple soul
I'm turning yellow
like the rosemary flower.

*—Federico Garicia Lorca*

When you want to commemorate an occasion, a person, or something particularly special, this combination of flowers comes together to create an everlasting impression. Pink carnations, meaning "I will always remember you," are represented in abundance. Rosemary, meaning "remembrance" itself, is tucked in to add symbolic and visual depth. The addition of spearmint, meaning "warmth of sentiment" or "never forget," reinforces the importance of the memory. Small bunches of oak leaf hydrangea—meaning "dispassion" or in this context "calm"—are added for serenity. After all, the events of our lives come together to make us who we are. Sometimes sharp and other times blurred, memories can be elusive or seared into our minds forever.

## Ingredients

**I Will Always Remember You:** twelve stems
  dusty blush (pink) carnation
**Remembrance:** six sprigs rosemary
**Calm:** four stems green oak leaf hydrangea
**Warmth of Sentiment, Never Forget:** six
  sprigs spearmint

*Alternative botanicals:* blue periwinkle,
  calendula, forget-me-not, strawflower,
  white periwinkle

## To Create the Arrangement

1. This bouquet can be wrapped or placed in a tall vase once completed. Be sure to use only one color of carnation. Because they are inexpensive, an abundant amount can be included in the arrangement.

2. Begin by taking the carnations in one hand. Raise and lower some of the blooms so they are at varying heights and can all be seen. The stems at the bottom will be a mess, but for now, leave them because they will be trimmed at the end.

3. Next add the hydrangea stems, one by one, and insert them into the bouquet. Cluster one bunch into the top right and add some throughout the bouquet for visual balance.

4. Finally tuck in the rosemary and spearmint to add foliage, fragrance, and texture.

5. Tie the arrangement with a bow and then, once it's secure, trim the stems to a uniform length.

> *Tip: Always cut carnations just above one of the nodes (bumps on the stalk) to give them an easier opportunity to absorb water. Also, let the season inspire your color palette. For example, pastels are fitting for spring and golden sunset colors to celebrate autumn.*

Flowers seem intended for the
solace of ordinary humanity…

—John Ruskin, "On Leaf
Beauty: Leaves Motionless,"
Modern Painters, 1843

# SMITTEN

It's the time that you spent on your rose that makes your rose so important…
People have forgotten this truth, but you mustn't forget it. You become responsible
forever for what you've tamed. You're responsible for your rose.

*—Antoine de Saint-Exupéry*

The heady scent and vibrant color of the orange roses, meaning "fascination," combine with the dappled, ethereal leaves of maidenhair fern, meaning "secrecy," to enchant and bewitch in this lush bouquet. The pink geranium adds visual and textural beauty and shows that "preference" is given to the receiver of the arrangement. This botanical combination can be a powerful way to clandestinely express your feelings for someone who holds you in their thrall.

## Ingredients

**Secret Fascination:** five stems orange spray roses and rose buds
**Secrecy:** five stems maidenhair fern
**Preference:** three stems pink geranium

*Alternative botanicals:* acacia, apple/apple blossom, bachelor button/cornflower, calendula, canary grass, China aster, clove, cyclamen, fern, gladiola, honey flower, juniper, motherwort, Niphetos rose, orange rose, peony, pink geranium, rose, yellow acacia

## To Create the Arrangement

1. Begin with a ceramic vase with a narrow opening. Place a small pin frog secured with putty in the vase. If the opening is too small to get your hand into the vase, arrange a couple of rose stems onto the pin frog outside of the vase. Then place the putty on the bottom of the frog and insert it into the vase using the rose stems to press down and secure the frog.

2. Next, trim the rose stems to varying lengths, shorter than the first roses that were placed, and cluster them. Don't worry if the pin frog is full at this point. It was used as a foundation but doesn't need to be used to support the additional flowers.

3. Remove most of the leaves from the stems of the geranium, leaving the top leaves for filler. Place them next to each cluster.

4. Finally, tuck in the fern around the edges to give a cascading look and then tuck additional stems into the bouquet, allowing the foliage to pop out to add texture and flutter.

> *Tip: When creating an arrangement for your home, think about where it will be displayed. If on a table center, it should be visually appealing all the way around. If it will sit up against a wall, focus the flowers forward and to the left and right and choose colors that pop against the wall color.*

Whoever understands
life loves flowers and
their innocent caresses.

—*Auguste Rodin*

# STRENGTH

Yet nor the lays of birds nor the sweet smell

Of different flowers in odour and in hue

Could make me any summer's story tell,

Or from their proud lap pluck them where they grew.

*—William Shakespeare*

A vintage watering can is the perfect vessel to symbolize the strength that comes with time, but this arrangement can also be given as a wrapped bouquet or assembled in a more traditional vase. The focus flowers for "strength" come in the form of ginger and coneflower. And remember, strength doesn't necessarily mean "sturdy." It is also represented in the mighty-yet-delicate fennel with its wispy greens, which are both delicate and tough. Yarrow, eucalyptus, and protea are tucked in to bring complexity in the form of courage, bravery, and protection.

## Ingredients

**Strength:** one stem ginger
**Strength:** five stems purple echinacea
  (coneflower)
**Courage:** four stems protea
**Strength, Worthy of Praise:** three
  stems fennel
**Bravery, Protection, Power:** five stems
  cottage mix yarrow

**Protection:** five stems baby blue eucalyptus
**Independence:** three stems blue erygium
  (see holly)

*Alternative botanicals:* black poplar, borage,
  cedar, chamomile, edelweiss, French willow,
  gladiola, mullein, oak, peony, red or burgundy
  astrantia, succulent, sweet William

## To Create the Arrangement

1. This arrangement was built using a hand-tied method (see page 42) but with the intent of being placed into an antique watering can. Before beginning, take a close look at the vessel you choose so you don't accidentally create an arrangement too wide to fit the opening.

2. Be sure to remove the lower leaves before you begin so you don't have to set down the bouquet to work on the stems during the process. Also, cut the twine and place the length of it over your shoulder so it's handy and available when you need it.

3. The ginger is the base of this bouquet because the stems are thick.

4. Next alternate the additional flowers, a few stems at a time. Add stems, twist, add stems, and twist. This method allows the blooms to open and have plenty of space.

5. Once you like how the bouquet looks, secure the base of the stems with twine.

6. Trim the stems to the length of the shortest stem to ensure that all of them, once placed in the vessel, will be in the water.

7. Fill the vessel three-quarters full of water and place the bouquet into the vessel.

> *Tip:* Don't hold yourself hostage to various rules regarding flowers versus their vessel size. While I typically lean toward the vessel height being smaller than the height of the botanical arrangement it holds, when you find a vessel that speaks to you, run with it.

O, these I lack,

To make you garlands of, and my sweet friend,

To strew him o'er and o'er!'

—*William Shakespeare*

# SUCCESS

"Being natural is simply a pose, and the most irritating pose I know,"
cried Lord Henry, laughing; and the two young men went out into the garden
together and ensconced themselves on a long bamboo seat that stood in the shade
of a tall laurel bush.

—*Oscar Wilde*

The laurel leaf has been the symbol of success since the Roman era. It was worn as a symbol of glory and achievement by those who used their knowledge to serve the public in beneficial and honorable ways. The garland made of laurel, meaning "success," and intertwined with sage, meaning "virtue," is the perfect decoration to adorn a home during the holidays to symbolize the success of the year past and ring in a bountiful new year. It can also ornament a table as a festive centerpiece to ensure a successful dinner party or hang above a door at a graduation celebration.

## Ingredients

**Success:** ten branches laurel, cut into smaller sections

**Virtue:** one bunch broadleaf sage, divided

*Alternative botanicals:* allium, beech, laurel, nasturtium, spirea, wheat

## Seasonal Ingredient Additions

**Winter**—St. John's wort buds (truth, protection), dried orange slices (abundance, happiness)

**Spring**—blue Monday sage (virtue), blue globe eryngium (independence)

**Summer**—pink sage (virtue), strawflower (everlasting, agreement)

The Love Language of Flowers

**Autumn**—wheat (prosperity), orange wax flower (enduring wealth, riches)

## To Create the Arrangement

1.  Begin with a spool of medium-weight floral wire (the thicker the garland, the heavier the gauge needed).

2.  Trim the stems into sections approximately six inches (fifteen cm) long and create an even number of laurel and sage bundles.

3.  Choose a bundle with an attractive top to act as the first end of the garland and secure floral wire to it by twisting the wire around the stems three times. Do not cut the floral wire. Leave it attached to its paddle, unrolling it as you move down the garland.

4.  Next, attach additional bundles (one at a time), slightly overlapping them, winding the wire in a spiral direction and weaving it between the leaves so the wire winds directly around the main branch of each piece of laurel.

5.  Once you have reached the halfway point of your garland, switch directions so that the bundles are now facing away from the section of garland you just completed. To do this, lay the end of your next bundle on top of the end of the previous bundle, overlapping them so the greenery is nearly touching, and wind the wire around to secure them together several times.

6.  Continue attaching the remaining bundles until the two halves are generally equal in length. Your final laurel branch should have a full and round end to finish the garland.

> *Tip: Anchoring the center of your garland with seasonal details adds visual interest and hides the hardware where the two halves split directions.*

Narcissus falls in love
with his own shadow,
which he sees in a
fountain; and, pining to
death, the Gods change
him into a flower, which
still bears his name.

—*Ovid*

# THANKFULNESS

Perhaps you'd like to buy a flower?

But I could never sell.

If you would like to borrow

Until the daffodil

Unties her yellow bonnet

Beneath the village door,

Until the bees, from clover rows

Their hock and sherry draw,

Why, I will lend until just then,

But not an hour more!

—Emily Dickinson

This arrangement symbolizes the gratitude that can be found in even the simplest things. Giving flowers to show a sense of thankfulness is one of the most pleasurable bouquets to deliver. The rich, golden-hued calendula, signifying "thankfulness," is the focus flower and is at the base of the arrangement to show that being thankful is the foundation and primary sentiment of the floral design. Canaliculatis, or mini daffodils, adds a sense of cheer to bring an extra element of joyful gratitude. Stems of geranium leaves, signifying "friendship," adds color and texture to the arrangement. This arrangement can also be created for yourself as a reminder to be thankful for all the people and joy in your life.

## Ingredients

**Regard, New Beginning:** five stems mini daffodil, plus one stem standard-sized daffodil
**Friendship:** two stems geranium leaves
**Thankfulness:** four stems Pacific Beauty calendula

*Alternative botanicals:* bellflower/campanula, dianthus, lisianthus

## To Create the Arrangement

1. This simple arrangement has a refined look, almost like Ikebana (which means the Japanese art of flower arrangement). Begin with a shallow bowl and place a pin frog secured with floral putty, which is especially important when using a shallow bowl.

2. Fill the bowl three-quarters of water and then begin by placing the mini daffodils, stem by stem, and secure them into the pin frog toward the back half. Leave some of the greenery on the stems for additional texture and color.

3. Next, cut the stems of the Pacific Beauty calendula so that the height of the blooms will be below the daffodil blooms. Then place them into the front half of the frog.

4. Finally, to add a sense of balance, trim the stem of the full-size daffodil to approximately three inches and then place it on the bottom right. It also serves to cover the pin frog.

> *Tip: Daffodils release a harmful sap that causes the water to brown and, therefore, should not share water with other flowers. To address this, isolate daffodil stems by securing them in their own test tube of water or use floral water tubes/vials. Alternatively, you can soak your daffodil stems in a gallon of water with ¼ teaspoon of bleach for six to twelve hours prior to creating your arrangement. This should remove the sap from the stems.*

I look for myself but find no one.
I belong to the chrysanthemum
hour of bright flowers placed in
tall vases. I should make
an ornament of my soul.

—*Fernando Passoa*

# TRUTH

Every year, in November, at the season that follows the hour of the dead,
the crowning and majestic hours of autumn, I go to visit the chrysanthemums…
They are indeed, the most universal, the most diverse of flowers.

*—Maurice Maeterlinck*

Sometimes a special occasion calls for a show of truth and sincerity. Perhaps you want to reveal your true character or reveal a personal vulnerability to a friend or someone you love. Or you want to show that your intentions are pure. The focus flower of this arrangement, chrysanthemum, meaning "truth," provides the structural and emotional foundation. Springs of mint, representing "virtue," are included to symbolize honor and the importance of showing your inner truth.

## Ingredients

**Truth:** eight stems purple chrysanthemum, variety of tones and sizes

**Virtue:** five sprigs mint

*Alternative botanicals:* allium, anemone, chrysanthemum, honesty/lunaria, white chrysanthemum

## To Create the Arrangement

1. For this arrangement, similar vessels, placed in a line, create a dramatic effect and are perfect for a long table or a dinner party where people are passing food and chatting.

2. To begin, strip the bottom leaves off the chrysanthemum of varying colors and shapes. Before building the mini bouquets, note the variations in color, so each has variety.

3. Add a similar number of blooms to each, varying the heights slightly but not dramatically.

4. Tuck sprigs of mint into each bouquet for a lovely scent and a bit of color.

5. For the table settings, because sword fern also means truth, add one to the place setting. Place a single chrysanthemum on top of each fern for a pop of color and to tie into the arrangement.

*Tip: When creating an arrangement acting as a centerpiece, make sure it has visual interest from all sides and angles and that it does not reach above the shoulders of guests seated at the table.*

# Sources

## Fresh Botanicals

**Down To Earth Snoqualmie**
8096 Railroad Ave, Snoqualmie, WA 98065
www.snoqualmieflowers.com
Family-owned and operated florist and
gift shop located in the heart of historic
downtown Snoqualmie.

**Mayesh Wholesale Florists Inc. Seattle**
663 S Orcas St, Seattle, WA 98108
www.mayesh.com/wa-seattle
Seattle wholesale flower distributor focused
on high-end boutique flowers and sourcing the
most unusual product from around the world.

**Seattle Wholesale Growers Market Cooperative**
665 S Orcas St, Seattle WA 98108
seattlewholesalegrowersmarket.com
Farmer-owned cooperative committed to
providing the best the Pacific Northwest has to
offer in cut flowers, foliage, and plants.

## Seeds, Corms, Bulbs, and Tubers

**Baker Creek Heirloom Seeds**
www.rareseeds.com
North America's largest heirloom seed
company keeping heirloom varieties alive for
future generations.

**Eden Brothers**
www.edenbrothers.com
Offers a large assortment of high-quality flower
seeds, bulbs, and perennials.

**Floret Flowers**
www.floretflowers.com
A family-run flower farm and seed company,
specializing in unique, uncommon, and
heirloom flowers and education.

**Flourish Flower Farm**
www.flourishflowerfarm.com
A family-run farm dedicated to growing only
specialty and heirloom varieties—producing
high-quality, organic, fragrant blooms.

**Halden Garden**
haldengarden.com
A family-run company sourcing seeds and
bulbs from the best seed wholesales in the US
and Holland.

Roozen Gaarde Flowers & Bulbs
www.tulips.com
A family business growing more than a
thousand acres of tulips, daffodils, and irises
in Skagit Valley, Washington, and the official
sponsor of the Skagit Valley Tulip Festival.

# Education

### Bloom & Burn
Located in the Garden of England using
seasonal, locally grown flowers for styling,
workshops, and event design. Celebrating small
growers and sustainable design practices.

### Floret Flowers
www.floretflowers.com
A family-run flower farm and seed company
specializing in unique, uncommon, and
heirloom flowers and education.

### Flourish Flower Farm
www.flourishflowerfarm.com
A family-run farm dedicated to growing only
specialty and heirloom varieties—producing
high-quality, organic, fragrant blooms.

# Vases & Vessels

### Ball Mason Jars
www.ballmasonjars.com

### Country Roads Antiques and Garden
216 W Chapman Ave, Orange, CA 92866
countryroadsantiques.com

### Etsy
www.etsy.com
An excellent worldwide source for vintage
flower frogs and vessels.

### Snohomish Antiques District
Snohomish, WA

### The Vintage Flea
33511 SE Redmond Fall City Rd,
Fall City WA 98024

# Acknowledgments

**Jess:** It is with the most grateful heart that I acknowledge Lisa McGuinness for trusting me with her vision for this book and Jessica Faroy for stumbling upon my account while digging through the depths of social media and believing I was someone worth exploring. Thank you to Elina Diaz for her brilliant design of the book. Thanks also to my late Grandma Brisboe, who walked me around her backyard, with my skinned knees and pigtails, showing me how beautiful it was to grow things. Most importantly, I want to acknowledge my husband, my biggest fan and best friend, who single-handedly built me the backyard garden of my dreams, where many of the flowers in this book grew. His unwavering support of my passion for gardening, writing, and photography gave me the confidence to accept this project and create from my heart.

**Lisa:** I am grateful to have found Jess Buttermore, whose photography allowed us to create the book I always dreamed of producing. She has been an excellent partner and brought not only extensive floral knowledge, but also an incredibly lovely floral sensibility to the table. Thanks also to Jessica Faroy for sourcing many of the wonderful quotes and lore found in this book. Huge gratitude goes to Elina Diaz for the beautiful design. And, most importantly, thank you to my wonderful Scottish granny, Alice Duncan, for instilling in me a love of gardening and a true appreciation of flowers.

# About the Author & Photographer

**Jess Buttermore** lives with her husband and three children in a small town nestled in the mountains of Seattle, Washington. Their homestead, Cedar House Farm, is her sanctuary where she enjoys gardening, herbalism, farming, baking, reading, photography, and crafting.

Jess has authored feature articles in *Click* magazine (issue 42), *Willow & Sage* magazine (Spring 2022, Winter 2023), *GreenCraft* magazine (Summer 2022), and *Obaahima* magazine (Volume 3 and Volume 4), various articles, recipes, and photography featured in Herbal Academy's resource materials, including the *Holiday Maker's Magazine*, and her photography has been featured in National Geographic's *Your Shot*, among many other online photography publications. She was named one of the Top 100 Photographers to Watch by Click & Co. in 2018, is a Click Pro Elite Member and Click & Co. Lifetime Member, and her photography has been featured in various exhibits and collections over the years.

Jess shares her gardening journey and intentional season living at www.cedarhouseliving.com and www.instagram.com/cedarhouseliving.

# About the Author

**Lisa McGuinness** is the author of *Catarina's Ring*, *Meaningful Bouquets*, *Hoppy Trails*, and *Caffeinated Ideas Journal* and the co-author of numerous children's books, including the *New York Times* bestselling *Bee & Me*. She is the CEO of the South East Asia Rescue Coalition & Haven (SEARCH) at search4hope.com, and often travels to SE Asia, where she volunteers in a safe house for women and children. For her day job, she's the Creative Director of Mango Publishing and works with designers, editors, and authors. Lisa has two grown children and one grandchild and lives in Northern California with her husband, Matt, and two hilarious dachshund mix dogs, Hazel and Wyatt.

yellow pear 🍐 press

Yellow Pear Press, established in 2015, publishes inspiring, charming, clever, distinctive, playful, imaginative, beautifully designed lifestyle books, cookbooks, literary fiction, notecards, and journals with a certain *joie de vivre* in both content and style. Yellow Pear Press books have been honored by the Independent Publisher Book (IPPY) Awards, National Indie Excellence Awards, Independent Press Awards, and International Book Awards. Reviews of our titles have appeared in Kirkus Reviews, Foreword Reviews, Booklist, Midwest Book Review, San Francisco Chronicle, and New York Journal of Books, among others. Yellow Pear Press joined forces with Mango Publishing in 2020, with the vision to continue publishing clever and innovative books. The fact that they're both named after fruit is a total coincidence.

We love hearing from our readers, so please stay in touch with us and follow us at:

Facebook: Mango Publishing
Twitter: @MangoPublishing
Instagram: @MangoPublishing
LinkedIn: Mango Publishing
Pinterest: Mango Publishing
Newsletter: mangopublishinggroup.com/newsletter